Twenty-Four
TEDDY BEARS
A Christmas Journey

We gratefully acknowledge the financial support of the Canada Council for the Arts, the Government of Canada through the Canada Book Fund (CBF), and the Government of Newfoundland and Labrador through the Department of Tourism, Culture and Recreation for our publishing program.

Printed on acid-free paper
Cover Design by Todd Manning
Layout by Fenton Fortune

Published by
Creative Publishers
an imprint of CREATIVE BOOK PUBLISHING
a Transcontinental Inc. associated company
P.O. Box 8660, Stn. A
St. John's, Newfoundland and Labrador A1B 3T7

Printed in Canada by: Transcontinental Inc.

Library and Archives Canada Cataloguing in Publication

Templeton, Bruce, author
    Twenty-four teddy bears : a Christmas journey / Bruce Templeton.

ISBN 978-1-77103-096-0 (paperback)

    1. Christmas--Anecdotes. 2. Santa Claus--Anecdotes. 3. Hospitals--Newfoundland and Labrador--St. John's--Anecdotes. 4. Visiting the sick.
I. Title. II. Title: 24 teddy bears.

GT4985.T445 2016   394.2663   C2016-904014-3

Believe Buddy!

Twenty-four
TEDDY BEARS
A Christmas Journey

Bruce Templeton

Author of *The Man in the Red Suit*
and *The Man with the White Beard*

Santa Bruce 2016

CREATIVE PUBLISHERS

St. John's, Newfoundland and Labrador, 2016

"Need a reminder of the true meaning of Christmas? Find it here in these beautifully moving stories from the man in the red suit."

Alan Doyle,
author of *Where I Belong: Small Town to Great Big Sea*

DEDICATION

This book is dedicated to my aunt,
Margaret (Bunty) McDonald House
(February 27, 1917-March 4, 2016).

She offered to assist Santa every year
by putting the scarves on all the teddy bears.

She fit this task into her schedule of reading books on
her iPad and following the stock market every day
while knitting afghans for old people.

She was a wonderfully cheerful lady.

Twenty-four TEDDY BEARS
A Christmas Journey

Table of Contents

V.	Dedication
VIII.	Preface
X.	Introduction

December 1st	1	The Community Centres
December 2nd	5	Ronald McDonald House
December 3rd	9	The Teddy Bear Toss
December 4th	13	The Downtown St. John's Christmas Parade

19 *Santa's Faithful Supporters*

December 5th	23	The Seniors' Home
December 6th	27	General Rick Hillier and Teddy Bears
December 7th	29	Santa's visit to Bishop Abraham Elementary
December 8th	33	Breakfast with Santa in Kelly Park
December 9th	39	The Gathering Place
December 10th	43	The Dr. H. Bliss Murphy Cancer Care Centre
December 11th	49	The Kids Are All Heart
December 12th	51	Brighter Futures

55 *Santa's Mail Bag*

December 13th	59	Daybreak Parent and Child Centre
December 14th	63	The Murphy Centre Children's Christmas Party
December 15th	67	The Children's Rehabilitation Centre
December 16th	71	The John Howard Society
December 17th	75	The Tuckamore Youth Treatment Centre
December 18th	79	Richard Rogers & The Knights of Columbus

83 *The International Santa Claus Hall of Fame*

December 19th	87	The Flight to the North Pole
December 20th	93	The Contrasts
December 21st	97	Graysen
December 22nd	101	Fooled You, Santa!

The Knights of St. Nicholas

December 23rd	109	Christmas Eve in the Janeway: Michele
December 24th	115	Christmas Eve in the Janeway: Charlie
	123	Conclusion: Journey's End
	125	Acknowledgements

PREFACE
TWENTY-FOUR TEDDY BEARS

This book came into being because I want to share the true stories of how my friend Santa Claus and his partner St. Nicholas give away some of Santa's teddy bears to very special people and for very special reasons during Santa's visits in Newfoundland and Labrador. I will tell you all about where the bears come from, how the Santa visits unfold and how the recipients are selected. Then, I will ask you to share with me the experience of giving the teddies away.

Yes, I have written two previous books about my friend Santa, but this one is different. It takes us into the history and symbolism of teddy bears, and, most importantly, the stories of some children and families who find themselves in challenging circumstances.

Over the years, many of the teddy recipients or family members have written or called me sometime later. They have told me what it was like to be in a room, sometimes

Photo credit Celebrity Photo Studio

at the children's hospital, other times in a senior's home, when Santa came for a visit. They relate how it felt when they heard the bells and saw Santa walk in. For a very brief period, Santa made the "not so normal" seem "normal" again.

Pediatric nurses are human, too, and on Christmas Eve, sometimes they are just as emotional as the parents when

Santa, visiting the Pediatric Intensive Care Unit, receives the nod from a healthcare professional to indicate that "this is where teddy should stay." There are rules around privacy, and for very good reasons. But the staff know the facts and the patient's prognosis. I have a secret elf with me on Christmas Eve (my daughter, Dr. Christina Templeton) and sometimes she is the one who gives me the nod. You will read more about my "doctor daughter" as these stories unfold. All I know is that I have a very special teddy, "Santa's Own Teddy," and it must find the arms of someone who needs him.

I invite you to join me on an adventure. Come and travel with me for a few hours. Read the stories of the teddies and their new homes and the families that have received them, and, when you close the book, if you are lucky enough to be at home with your own family, give thanks, for that is the best fortune in the world.

Bruce Templeton
St. John's, NL
April, 2016

INTRODUCTION

Twenty-four Teddy Bears is the story of how, over thirty-seven years, Santa, in St. John's, Newfoundland, has distributed hundreds of teddy bears. Some chapters also include comments from some of the families who have received them.

Santa has a wonderful supporter, who has asked to simply remain Elf 342, who owns several retail stores. She attends trade shows, and each year, around March or April, I get a simple email: "Teddies secured." This means that in late October, I will be called to a certain location and into my truck will be placed a large box containing a season's worth of teddy bears. "Off you go, Santa," is my donor's directive. We have done this together for a long time. Thank you Elf 342. Santa and St. Nicholas could not do their work without you, and hundreds of your bears are now in new homes.

My second stop is to my embroiderer, who makes the teddies' scarves. These have been various colours but are usually red with a winter character, like a snowman, sewn onto one end. On the other end, she inscribes "Santa's Own Teddy," and the year. As with my teddy supplier, I simply get a call: "The scarves are ready, Santa. Come and get them."

Finally, the components make their visit to my cousin Heather, my sister, Marian and, until this past spring, my ninety-nine-year-old Aunt Bunty, who would spend several hours removing the manufacturer's tags and getting the teddies dressed. My family looks forward to their part in making sure that Santa is ready to roll. Unfortunately, Aunt Bunty passed quietly away while this book was being written. I dedicate this book to her, in thanks.

The bears then come back to my house and are placed on a big shelf. Over the next twenty-five days the bears travel with Santa inside his mail bag where two Velcro straps go snuggly around the teddies' chests just under their arms. This allows teddy to peek out and see what is happening, but at the same time, prevents their falling out of the helicopter or the sleigh. Santa always knows how many visits are scheduled and how many bears to bring.

Before we start out on our teddy bear adventures, let's take a brief look back at how these little bears came to be, and what they came to mean.

Educators sometimes call teddy bears a "transitional item:" Something soft, like a blanket or a stuffed toy, which takes importance around a child's fourth or sixth month, as they move towards the external world, while still needing a cuddling sensation reminiscent of a parent's warm arms. Kindergarten teachers often see children coming into class hugging these items.

The teddy bear can be traced back to U.S President Theodore Roosevelt (1858-1919) and a hunting trip he took in Mississippi in November, 1902. After three days of hunting, other members of the party had acquired bears, but not Roosevelt. What to do? The president's bear hunt would be a failure! The hunting guides tracked down an old black bear that the dogs had trailed quite a distance. They tied the bear to a willow tree and called for the president. But Roosevelt took one look at the old bear and refused to shoot it. He felt doing so would be unsportsmanlike. Word of this hit newspapers across the country, and a political cartoonist, Clifford Berryman, drew a cartoon showing President Roosevelt refusing to shoot the bear. It ran in the *Washington*

Post on November 16, 1902, forever connecting bears with President Roosevelt.

So, where did the first plush toys come from? A Brooklyn, New York, candy shop owner, Morris Michtom, saw Berryman's original illustration and had an idea. Placing two stuffed toy bears, which his wife, Rose, had made, in his shop window, Michtom asked Roosevelt's permission to call these toy bears "teddy's bears." They quickly proved so popular Michtom and his wife started a toy company.

The rest is history. From their origin in a Mississippi hunting trip in 1902, teddy bears have never lost their comforting appeal.

CHAPTER ONE

THE COMMUNITY CENTRES

DECEMBER 1ST

Santa loves his visits to the community centres for many reasons. These are usually pretty big gatherings where there could be 100 children or more, all held in large gymnasiums or halls. In many cases, the buildings are in the centre of multi-unit social housing projects where there may be single parents, hard-working couples juggling low-paying jobs or perhaps new Canadians seeking shelter at a reasonable cost. The children in the area find great friendships in their peer groups and gather at the community centres where well-organized programs involving sports, crafts, skills development, or the arts are offered.

Santa's experience is that the age range is usually five to ten year olds, and this presents certain challenges. You know when you walk through the door that you will be affectionately mobbed by curious children! You also know that while there may be 100 children in the room, it is likely that there will only be a few volunteers and sometimes a couple of young people in their mid-teens to assist during the visit.

As Santa gets out of the sleigh, he double-checks that everything is strapped down tight before he walks through the doors and the fun starts! They are wonderful children who surround you, and they are not shy. Many have been there for years and they also know that Santa might take off his hat and place it on a child. But it still doesn't prepare you for the surprise of the mischievous youngster who sneaks up from behind you and whips off your hat, puts it on their head and parades around the room claiming to be Santa's assistant. But it is all in good fun; you just need to be ready.

The organizers usually have the resources to buy a gift for each of the children. Sometimes these kids may not receive much at home at Christmas, so these gifts are appreciated.

The volunteers at the events get very experienced at the gift distribution. If there are 100 excited and impatient children all sitting on the floor, and if each child takes a minute with Santa, then we are looking at 100 minutes. That means more than an hour and a half for them all to be called to come to Santa.

Over the years, the volunteers have learned to be efficient. For example, they may divide the children by age and then take each group into a room. Thus, the children aged five and six may be in one group with Santa while the others are playing a game or eating a hotdog. Then the groups shift after fifteen minutes and the next comes for their visit. Frequently, brothers or sisters are there for a child who is sick and Santa gives them the child's gift to be taken home. All of these procedures develop from years of experience at these very large visits.

Pictures are usually taken at the end of each age group and family photos at the close of the event. Santa has lots of time and he knows, with this number of children, the visit could take several hours.

Santa has been coming to one particularly large centre for many years and the organizers tell this true story that happened many years ago. As the program director tells it:

It was a cold and snowy day when the children's party was held and there was lots of excitement in anticipation of Santa walking through the door. The staff, children and parents can quickly sense the change of atmosphere. It's difficult to say for certain who is more excited for the man in the big red suit. The moment his bells and jolly laugh can be heard, the entire group falls quiet and patiently awaits his arrival. The attendance that day was over 100 children and all of the gifts were wrapped and under the tree. We pretty well knew the routine of Santa's visits and he brings two very important items. The first is his photo album, which he shows to the kids at the beginning of each visit, usually laying on the mats on the floor. The second item is a teddy bear and this bear is very important as well. The bear is given to one special child during each visit. There are many different reasons a child may be chosen to receive the bear and we nod to Santa to indicate who the recipient should be when he meets the child. For example, some years the child that has been chosen for Santa's teddy bear is part of a family who is experiencing a difficult time in their lives, whether financial hardship or the loss of a family member. Other years it has been because a child has made large improvements academically, or has had a positive impact on someone else's life.

Photo credit Kim Hart

3

But one year, the program director realized they'd made a mistake with the presents.

All of the children sat patiently on the floor as the gift distribution was started. There were so many children that two elves stood on either side of Santa and called the names. Other assistants handed them the gifts from under the tree. It moved along quite quickly. As time went on, the large throng of kids slowly thinned out— fifty, twenty-five, ten—as the children unwrapped their gifts and scattered.

Finally Santa heard, "All done, Santa," from behind the tree and organizers with big garbage bags were scooping paper and ribbon from the floor.

But Santa looked down from his big red chair and saw one little boy left, sitting with his fingers crossed. He had tears in his eyes. "Oh, Santa," whispered an elf. "That is Jacob. We didn't know he was coming and we don't have a gift for him. What will we do?"

Santa called his name. "Jacob, come and see Santa." The little boy came forward. "Jacob, every morning when Santa leaves the North Pole, the elves put a very special gift in my mail bag and they ask me to find a very special person to give it to. Look what I have for you! Will you look after my bear?" Santa took the teddy from the bag and gave it to his little friend. Jacob smiled. "Thank you, Santa. I promise to look after him forever."

The visit was complete.

That child is a twenty-year-old university student now. His friends must think him exceptional, for in the corner of his dorm room sits a teddy bear with a little red scarf that says "Santa's Own Teddy, 1999."

CHAPTER TWO

RONALD McDONALD HOUSE

DECEMBER 2ND

" I told you, Mommy. I told you. I told you that Santa would find us here at Ronald McDonald House!"

The little girl was standing in front of her mother with her arms down in front of her, palms out and her fingers spread wide. "I knew he would find us and look, here he is!"

Santa loves his visits to Ronald McDonald House Newfoundland and Labrador, and he has made many since the house opened. Despite the children's medical challenges, their greatest concern when staying there over Christmas is whether Santa will know they are at Ronald McDonald House and not at home. The children's hospital makes a great effort to ensure that every child who can go home does go home, and of course it is the fondest wish of everyone on the staff of Ronald McDonald House that no child and family is required to be there over Christmas, but such is not always the case. As a matter of fact, children have been flown into the hospital and families have arrived at the house on Christmas Eve. The doors are always open to receive a sick child and their family.

Ronald McDonald House is a wonderful place. This house is on the grounds of the combined Health Sciences Centre and Janeway children's hospital. It can house fifteen families at any one time and everyone works very hard to make the stay as normal as possible. The food is "home-cooked" on-site by visiting local support groups like Rotary, and there are play areas, crafts, games, a library and an outside playground.

On Christmas Eve, Santa parked his sleigh in the snow and walked toward the building. A cheery Christmas tree cast its light on the very realistic, life-size Ronald McDonald sitting on a bench outside the building. Snowflakes gently and quietly covered the scene. Santa started to ring his bells, and inside the glass doors, red-and-green-dressed elves gathered to greet Santa. The big doors opened and the sights, sounds and smells of a beautiful Christmas house spilled out and enveloped Santa as he walked into the building.

There were Christmas trees, wreaths and garlands. A young musician strummed his guitar and children were singing. Large trays of cookies tempted Santa as he inhaled the cinnamon and chocolate scents. (Watch your diet, Santa! We have three weeks before the big day and the elves have a big meal for you when you get home tonight.)

Santa looked around the large living room door at the children seated on the floor. The guest list has been expanded to include the volunteers, the supporting board and their families, and that adds to the feeling of normalcy that is vitally sought by the resident children. Sometimes you can see tubes, masks, bandages and wheelchairs, but generally all appears as it should.

Santa gets down on the floor and opens his photo album. The children follow Santa's progress at the Santa Claus Parade and other visits where photos were appropriate and permitted.

Then, the most precocious and outgoing child stepped up and pointed once again. She wore a little red dress, and her curly hair was topped with a sprig of holly on her headband. "Look Mommy, look! I told you he would find us. I knew that he would know we were here at Ronald McDonald House." The children seem to be able to face anything in the hospital as they deal with the treatments and the medications – but as Christmas gets closer and closer, the staff must constantly remind the children that if by some chance they are still there at Christmas, Santa will find them and that he does know where they are – that's their worry.

Santa took the teddy out of his mail bag and handed it to our little believer. This little girl had apparently been admitted with what was thought to be a simple problem, but nine months later, was receiving treatment for an aggressive condition.

This is the great value of Ronald McDonald House. It brings relief and solicitude to parents who can stay within minutes of the hospital while finding the rest and the support that the house gives them as primary caregivers. While the staff obviously know when a family is checking into the house, they really don't know when one is checking out. Yes, they have seen families happily skipping down the driveway and waving goodbye to Ronald, but they have also seen couples walk away in shock and disbelief, holding one another as they face the future without their child.

Santa waved to the children and walked out into the snowy driveway.

Look after the children, St. Nicholas. These precious gems are our future.

CHAPTER THREE

THE TEDDY BEAR TOSS

DECEMBER 3RD

Imagine standing at centre ice at Mile One Stadium on New Gower Street in St. John's during the second intermission of an AHL hockey game. Yes, this is the home of the IceCaps, the AHL affiliate of the Montreal Canadiens team. You look up, and all around you there are 7,000 people in the seats, many sporting their favourite hockey jersey and some are moving down the aisles to the perimeter glass. Standing beside you, waving, is the amazing mascot for the St. John's IceCaps, "Buddy the Puffin."

So what is this all about? This is the "Teddy Bear Toss," which happens every year, one component of the IceCaps' community support.

Hockey game intermissions are only twenty minutes long. A big flow of people, led by the Salvation Army, flood onto the ice. From the Zamboni corner, four or five vehicles edge their way onto the ice surface.

The stadium announcer starts his countdown: "Five-four-three-two-one," and then teddy bears start to rain down; hundreds and hundreds of teddy bears come flying out of the stands, over the glass and bouncing and sliding onto the ice. Santa ducks as a bear zings past his head, and Buddy opens his big gloves and catches as many bears as he can. Soon, you can hardly see the ice surface, and still they come from the rafters and the boxes high up in the building. Then the ice crew starts herding the teddies towards the vehicles until these are stuffed to the roof with bears of every size

and colour. With less than ten minutes to prepare for the resumption of play, the vehicles exit the building and the Zambonis go about their work. Outside the rink, there is a large box truck from the Salvation Army and, one at a time, the smaller vehicles disgorge the armloads of bears into the larger one. Buddy and Santa are inside it as it is filled and the bears reach the roof in no time. How many bears are there? The guess is about four thousand.

As Santa is about the leave the truck, he reaches for his mail bag and for his own teddy. While there may be thousands of bears in the truck, there is only one with a little red scarf that says "Santa's Own Teddy." Santa turns, and together, he and Buddy throw him into the pile. "So long my friend. Make a child happy somewhere." The big door is closed and the truck edges out onto the street with its precious cargo.

(Later in the month, the very committed members of the Salvation Army distribute more than 1,700 bears to registered families throughout Newfoundland and Labrador. The assistance may include food hampers, as well.)

It has been a busy night for us all. Santa arrived at the stadium at 6 p.m. and was out in the atrium box office area with Buddy, having photos taken with children right up until game time at 7:30 p.m. The lines were long and the children were thrilled because Buddy is a very popular bird! Then, between the first and second periods of the game, hundreds more children posed for photos.

About 10 p.m., Santa shakes hands with Buddy and heads back to the North Pole. While the North Pole team works awfully hard, it is sure nice to know that the wonderful IceCaps, with their mascot, Buddy, and the folks from the Salvation Army all become Santa's elves for one big night in December.

But the work of the Salvation Army never ends. Throughout the year, they will respond to those in need. An ice-jam may block a river and flood homes upstream. A windstorm can blow roofs off homes in its path. Forest fires can thunder down a hillside and burn the homes of those who live below. It is the Salvation Army who will likely be amongst the first responders, and, in their emergency vehicles of blankets and food, there is a supply of teddy bears.

Tonight, thanks to the Salvation Army, Santa's bear is out there somewhere in the arms of a child, along with the thousands of bears from the generous, loyal fans of the IceCaps.

CHAPTER FOUR

THE DOWNTOWN ST. JOHN'S CHRISTMAS PARADE

DECEMBER 4TH

"Wakey, wakey, Santa, it is 6 a.m. and they need you for a call in an hour from St. John's, Newfoundland." Santa waved to his wonderful elf, who then went and put on the coffee pot. Santa tiptoed to the shower and let Mrs. Claus sleep in.

After his breakfast, the call came. "Hi Santa, this is Gaylynne from the Downtown St. John's Christmas Parade. The weather here is beautiful and the parade is a go. We will expect your helicopter at noon and our crew is all ready to pick you up."

The Downtown St. John's Christmas Parade is a wonderful event. It takes months of planning and cooperation from many groups. The parade committee has its final pre-parade meeting at 7 a.m. at a local restaurant where, following a long consultation with the weather office, the final decision is made. "Clear in the morning and a light snowfall starting when Santa lands! Temperature about zero and no wind." Perfect!

The committee then executes its plan. Mill fencing (temporary protective metalwork) is erected where any hazard exists. Road closure barriers are placed strategically. "No Parking" yellow hoods, set over parking meters the afternoon before, are double-checked. Media towers for television crews are erected, and the reviewing stand for the dignitaries is pulled into place.

At the marshalling area, the long lines are set out with placement markers and, as the floats arrive, the parade officials arrange them in order. Heated buses arrive early and park so that dance groups, costumed characters and cheerleaders can stay warm until just before they are due to march out with bands and sound trucks. Emergency vehicles are in place, including tow trucks, police cars and the St. John Ambulance personnel. It takes hours and hours of preparation but the leadership from the office of Downtown St. John's has everything planned that can be planned.

At 10 a.m., the helicopter arrives in the North Pole and Santa is ready. We lift off and head southeast toward Newfoundland and Labrador. While the reindeer can fly at the speed of light, Santa's helicopter isn't quite as fast, but we do arrive at the heliport in time for Santa to make his first stop with guests from the Janeway Children's Rehabilitation Centre (as told in Chapter 8).

At noon, the helicopter lifts off again and we head for the parade route. If it is a nice day, the door is removed and, as we have a low-flight permit, the children can clearly see that Santa has arrived. The pilot skilfully traverses the route several times and then hovers. From that height, we can see the whole parade as it gears up to depart the parking lot, led by employees of Newfoundland Power, who accept donations for the Community Food Sharing Association along the downtown route (in the past, upwards of ten tonnes of food has been collected). Then we spot the four big, black horses of the Royal Newfoundland Constabulary and we know the parade is underway.

The chopper makes a wide swing and the pilot lands gently. Santa emerges, as does Mrs. Claus, identified only by her red hat and the microphone on her cheek, which allows her to talk to Santa while she walks the entire route just ahead of the sleigh. She has done this with Santa for more than thirty years.

What Mrs. Claus does is carefully approach the parents of a child (who may be sitting wrapped in blankets) and quietly ask, "What is your child's name?" Then she walks back into the centre of the road and Santa hears, "On your left, now, wrapped in pink blankets on the sidewalk, is Ashley." Santa turns to his left and looks down. Through the speakers mounted along the sleigh he says: "Merry Christmas, Ashley. You look nice and warm. I hope you have a wonderful Christmas." Ashley's parents join in the fun as an astonished child turns to face them. "He knows me! He knows me!"

The whole parade route is over two kilometres and the weather comes through exactly as the weather people said it would. It starts to snow great big flakes that float ever so gently on the crowd. The clowns dance, the cheerleaders perform their well-practised routines and the marching bands, all decked out for the big day, play and lead on.

Soon Santa can see the end, and there, too, is a special and now regular part of the parade. For many years, a little girl named MaKayla has been there when Santa steps out of his sleigh, comes down two sets of laddered steps and finally steps onto the ground. MaKayla's mother is a very important elf and has been associated with the parade for many years. One year, Santa's teddy bear went to this very wonderful elf, selected from all those who were at the parade. A few years later, McKayla took home a bear of her own.

Let me end this chapter with her mother's words:

People tend to forget the real reason of Christmas. I have known Santa for many years and when I see him in

his suit, glasses, watch, bells and hat, there is a magic in the air. I always say that he would make anyone believe if they didn't. Since my daughter was born in 2003, she has told me many times that there is only one real Santa. He is the Santa that her mommy knows from the Downtown St. John's Christmas Parade. The Santas at the malls, etc., are just Santa's helpers! She said that the real Santa is kind, friendly and he loves to get down and play with us on the floor.

Santa's teddies are legendary, and very special. I have my own teddy from Santa as does my daughter, MaKayla. When I received my very own teddy, I was beside myself because of all the people Santa could pick, it was me! It made me feel very happy, loved and I felt that I had a job to keep the teddy safe and love him like any child would do. MaKayla was born December 22, 2003, so she was my Christmas present. Since she has been born I have tried to make her birthdays special. Santa has been able to attend her parties from time to time. At one of those parties MaKayla got her own Santa's teddy. I have never seen my child so proud and happy.

I asked her once, 'What did it mean to you to get one of Santa's teddies?' This is what she wrote, 'To get one of Santa's own teddies made me feel special and more proud of myself. I felt special and warm-hearted because not a lot of kids get one of Santa's teddies. My heart felt as if I got $100. I don't know how but it makes me feel proud of myself. Sometimes I think I can't do stuff and I put myself down. But when I got a teddy it made me believe that I could do anything, the sky is the limit.'

I truly love Santa and Santa's magic teddies. They have soooo much meaning for everyone.

Thank you Santa for making children and adults like me feel the magic and helping us truly believe in the magic of Christmas!

Love,
Bernadette & MaKayla

SANTA'S FAITHFUL SUPPORTERS

A question frequently asked is, "how can you do that?" "How can you get a plane to fly children to the North Pole?" "How can you get helicopters to drop out of the sky and deliver Santa safely before astonished children?" or "how do you get the support of the business community to deliver milk and cookies to a whole school full of children?"

The answer is simply that you find the people who dream as big as you do and have the power and the authority to say "yes, we can do that."

Now, I will admit that sometimes Santa really does push the limits. Such was the case a number of years ago when he thought it would be a great thrill for the children if the helicopter, on which Santa flew into St. John's, was actually taken through the parade on the back of a small trailer. Santa would then wave goodbye and lift-off outside of City Hall in the middle of the main street!

When Santa first brought up the idea, his astonished supporters said "You want to do what, Santa!!?

I went to the helicopter company and learned what the obstacles were. The landing pad was a small trailer, which attached to the little open tractor you see at the airport moving baggage on and off planes. Neither tractor nor trailers are licensed to go on city streets. So I asked if they had a police escort front and back, could the equipment make its way to the landing site, go through the parade (once the rotor blades were folded back and secured) and then be escorted back to the heliport? They agreed that it could be done if I could get the police to agree. So off I went to see the chief!

"You want us to do what, Santa!!?" he asked. The chief has a big heart and his own children. "Sure, we can do that" he agreed.

Now what about Transport Canada and permission to land in the city, and then later lift off in a chopper with children up the sides of a very high hill, with wires, poles and trees just outside City Hall? I wisely left that to the elves at Universal Helicopters and I think even to their surprise, permission was granted with the proviso that the chopper be back at the landing pad before dark! (That suited the police because there were no tail lights on the landing pad trailer!)

Did we do it? Of course we did. And people still remember it today, twenty years later.

The Flight to the North Pole with Provincial Airlines (PAL) and 99.1 Hits FM radio is an event that requires hours of staff time and a full flight crew and fuel to create a lifelong memory for children. How could you ever forget, if you were five or six years old, that your parents got you out of bed and took you to the airport before 6 a.m. to fly and meet Santa. Thank you PAL and the team from Steele Communications. You are amazing to work with.

The wonderful people at Newfoundland Power said "yes" when Santa and the parade organizers at Downtown St. John's asked them to send their employees along the route and push supermarket carts to collect food from the 60,000 people who attend. Over the years, tons and tons of food have gone to the Community Food Sharing Association at that critical time before Christmas.

Thank you to the media and the team at NTV who televise the parade and rebroadcast it several times. They are also at centre ice with Santa at the "teddy toss" during the AHL hockey game.

Bell Mobility steps up every year to provide the communication equipment so that Mrs. Claus, faithfully walking the parade route now for more than thirty years, can talk to Santa at the top of the sleigh with the names of the children sitting at road side. And what a delight it is when Santa looks directly at them, greets them by name and wishes them a "Merry Christmas."

Elf 342 is a local business owner who has supplied Santa's teddy bears for many years. She quietly makes the donation and asks for nothing more. Then Santa's embroidery supplier makes the little scarves and this company, as well, only asks that a sample bear come early in July so that the work can be done over the summer.

The story goes on and on. Santa gave milk and cookies to a whole school full of children because a Rotary elf bought these supplies in response to a child's question. "Mommy says there is no money for milk and cookies. Does Santa only go to the houses where there is milk and cookies?"

Thank you to the whole business community and to the Downtown St. John's organization because, without your efforts, the Santa Claus Parade would never happen and memories would stay in fantasy and dreams.

Chapter Five

The Seniors' Home

December 5th

Santa loves his visits to the seniors' homes. These large complexes contain many features designed to meet the medical and social needs of the residents. There are spacious dining rooms, libraries, small cinemas, beauty parlours and even podiatrists and pharmacies.

In addition, some contain nursery schools and daycares which give seniors the great opportunity to interact with small children. Many facilities host events which bring in musicians, storytellers and entertainers, too. Visits from dog groups are also something seniors enjoy, with many recalling the pets that they had years ago.

Some buildings offer multiple levels of care, usually numbered 1 through 3, establishing the extent of service that a senior may need. Level 1 can go from calling for little or no help with mobility and being easily able to access the dining room, while Level 3 includes increasing levels of medical and personal care.

Santa is invited for his annual visit and brunch, held in the big dining room on the main floor, decorated with red and green tablecloths, Christmas trees and holly. The residents invite their children and grandchildren and it is a lot of fun and very festive.

Usually a clown or magician spends some time baffling the kids or a balloon man has contorted long, multicolour balloons by twisting them into a requested character or animal. Then Santa arrives on the usual signal of "Here

Comes Santa Claus." The gifts are distributed and many ask to have family photos taken. Everyone is dressed in their Sunday best and grateful to be together for one more Christmas. No one knows what the next year will bring.

Once the main event is complete, the staff takes Santa from the dining area to the elevator and we head to the upper floors. Here things are very different. Many residents are bedridden. There may or may not be little Christmas trees in the rooms and there may or may not be cards that say, "We love you, Grandma." Some people are very frail, very thin and not very responsive.

Photo credit Templeton

On one occasion Santa was taking the elevator to the top floor, when its doors opened onto the reception area and he and his elves were met somewhat urgently by the floor's team leader.

"Santa, would you come immediately to Room 350? There is a woman who is dying and her family is there with her saying their final goodbyes."

Santa took a deep breath. I reached my left hand into the mail bag and held St. Nicholas. I quietly asked his advice.

"What should I do, Nicholas? How do I behave? Go before me, Nicholas. I will follow you."

We trooped down the hall. It seemed just a little surreal. We got to the doorway and looked inside. The living area was in view and the door to the bedroom was closed. Men and women sat in quiet vigil. The bedroom door opened and a woman (whom I later learned was the daughter of the resident) came out. With tears in her eyes, she said, "It won't be long now."

I took St. Nicholas from the mail bag and we talked briefly about how he was a very real priest. He dates from the fourth century and was a very caring, dedicated bishop and the patron saint of many, including children, students, teachers, sailors and repentant thieves.

Perhaps it was just something to take their minds away from the dreadful and sad circumstances, but the family members seemed to appreciate the brief visit from Santa and St. Nicholas.

When Santa stood to leave, he took his teddy from the mail bag and respectfully offered it to the daughter. She took it and said she would give it to her mother.

Santa left the room. We later learned that the resident passed away later in the afternoon.

Should Santa and St. Nicholas have gone into the room at all?

We were invited, and I believe that our presence brought comfort and reassurance.

CHAPTER SIX

GENERAL RICK HILLIER AND TEDDY BEARS

DECEMBER 6TH

Santa has met General Rick Hillier on many occasions and once we were fortunate enough to have a few quiet minutes to talk about teddy bears. General Hillier was Canada's Chief of Defence Staff from 2005 until 2008; he understood the great importance of keeping soldiers connected to Canada and to their families while they served away from home. This included inviting Canadian entertainers like Rick Mercer to perform for the troops; incorporating Tim Hortons coffee shops into the base infrastructure; and recruiting NHL players (with Stanley Cup in tow) for a game in Afghanistan. He also understood the power of teddy bears.

One year, General Hillier learned that there was a "recordable" teddy bear – when you pressed on the bear's paw and spoke, you could record a short message. He thought it would be a wonderful idea if a child at home could wake up on Christmas morning and hear the voice of their mother or father who was serving overseas. So, a quantity of bears was delivered to the troops and each soldier recorded a personal message. The bears were wrapped and transported back to Canada and delivered to the soldiers' homes.

What a thrill for a child on Christmas morning!

But then something happened that may not have been anticipated. One of the soldiers who had recorded a message to his family went out on patrol, triggered an improvised explosive device (IED) and died.

A message was sent to General Hillier that a teddy bear now carried a message from a fallen soldier. The bear was brought to him in Ottawa. After the family was informed of the soldier's death, General Hillier personally delivered the bear.[1]

CHAPTER SEVEN

SANTA'S VISIT TO BISHOP ABRAHAM ELEMENTARY

DECEMBER 7TH

What is it that makes a Santa visit to a certain elementary school, where there are 240 children in kindergarten to Grade 6, so memorable? Let me see if I can capture the spirit of this wonderful school.

For more than ten years, Santa has visited Bishop Abraham Elementary and his visit coincides with the last school assembly before the Christmas break. Santa makes this visit with a group of his travelling elves from the Rotary Club of St. John's East. These elves arrive with a special treat.

On the final day of school, the children are brought together in the gymnasium and the parents and guests are seated in chairs around the perimeter. The assembly happens in an orderly way as each grade arrives in turn; the little kindergarteners are the first to walk down the middle aisle to sit on the floor, and soon the whole school is together. The music teacher gets their attention and the program unfolds. Sometimes there is a skit which the teachers present; sometimes a class choir or a single student might perform. There have been years where a local children's entertainer has come along.

Part of the program might also include the reading of *'Twas the Night Before Christmas* and public officials have frequently been asked to do this. Thus, the children have gotten to see and meet lieutenant-governors, premiers and mayors. Whoever is invited, there are protocols to be

followed and timing is carefully considered. Santa is usually with the children prior to the dignitary's arrival. The children assemble at 9:50 a.m.; Santa comes at 9:55 a.m. and our guest reader at 10:00 a.m. We are all on the clock!

Santa's sleigh arrives in the parking lot at 9:30 a.m. and it is cold and windy. He puts his hand on the top of his head to hold his hat in place and leans into the wind as he proceeds up the driveway. He opens the first of the big double doors into the vestibule and waits for the fog that the sudden blast of heat forms on his glasses to slowly dissipate. With his eyesight clear, Santa views a huge new sign on the left wall. At the centre of the banner is the big word WELCOME. Then you see the children's painted faces and they are all different colours. Above or below each image is a greeting in a different language and a teacher explains that the school now has children from fifteen different countries. Santa is told that this year alone, more than a dozen children have come from Syria and three more are coming this week. At 3:15 p.m. each day, when the parents gather to pick up their children, there are multiple languages spoken in the vestibule.

At the appointed time, Santa starts to ring his bells and the gym doors open. With a loud "Ho, Ho, Ho!" Santa walks along the back where the parents are seated and then up the aisle through the children. The children are clapping and cheering but are wonderfully restrained. The teachers have done an amazing job preparing them and the children understand that rushing at Santa or pushing their classmates aside to be near him is not acceptable.

This year there was a special treat. As Santa came through the rows of parents, he saw a mother holding a sleeping infant and Santa stopped. "How old is the baby?" he inquired. "She is three weeks old, Santa, but she is really tiny," answered the mother. "Would you mind if Santa carried your baby and showed her to the children?" "No, of course not, Santa," so Santa gently took the baby and moved slowly up

Photo credit Terry Reardon

through the children, pausing and kneeling down so that the kids could see the little pink bundle he was holding. Then Santa returned the baby, who was still sound asleep, to her mother.

Soon, the principal announced the arrival of the lieutenant-governor and his wife, and the children were asked to stand. The vice-regal couple came through the doors with their aide-de-camp and they took their place at the front of the room. Their Honours greeted the children and everyone was seated. A child came forward with the book and softly asked His Honour if he would read them all a story. A quiet hush came over the whole gathering. Once the story was complete, Their Honours mingled with the children. Then the children all stood again and, starting with the kindergarten class, went quietly back to their classrooms.

Out in the hallway, Santa met his Rotary elves who had a large wagon full of milk and cookies. We went classroom to classroom and every child in the school was given this treat. As we went from class to class, we became even more aware of the great diversity amongst the students. In fact, many wondered, just who is this character in a red suit? And what is this event called Christmas all about?

Then we met two young girls in the hallway. "Santa, these are two of our recent arrivals from Eritrea, in East Africa. Say 'hi' to Feruz and Rahma." Santa greeted them both and a Rotary elf took a photo. After we had distributed milk and cookies to their class, a teacher nodded to signal Santa, who then reached into his mail bag and took out the teddy bear. Santa got down on one knee and held out the bear for Feruz to come forward. Her huge dark eyes widened and she smiled. "This is for you, Feruz, from Santa." She looked up and took the bear.

Tonight, Santa's teddy is learning a new language.

CHAPTER EIGHT

BREAKFAST WITH SANTA IN KELLY PARK

DECEMBER 8TH

One of the highlights of Santa's season is his visit to Outer Cove, and the annual Breakfast with Santa. It gets bigger every year. It is a very happy occasion and a chance to really have fun with the children. The breakfast is held in the community centre and, happily, a fenced ballfield is right out front. This is the second time each year when Santa asks his special elves at the helicopter company to fly him in.

I don't know what it would be like to be five or six years old, after you (and several hundred other children) have finished your pancakes, and suddenly you hear a thump-thump off in the distance. It must be fun as Mom or Dad put on your coat and boots and takes you out onto the balcony, just as a helicopter swoops overhead. You clap your hands over your ears!

Santa knows what it feels like as the pilot comes in low over the building and does a wide circle before landing in the swirling snow. Then, after the required four or five minutes to cool the engine and shut it down, Santa hops out and walks to the gate where the volunteers are keeping the children safely behind the fence. Along the way, Santa reaches down and scoops up a big handful of snow that he molds into a snowball. He throws it up into the air to land in the middle of the children. That is the only signal the kids need and soon snow is flying at Santa and the children are astonished that Santa has actually started a snowball fight.

The volunteers have been working for hours and hours getting ready. So, Santa has asked them to tell us in their words what it feels like:

Breakfast with Santa is unique. On the first Saturday of December each year the Town of Logy Bay–Middle Cove–Outer Cove prepares to host a breakfast for 220 residents and Santa Claus. As an organizer, often it is easy to get lost in the stream of logistics leading up the event. The list of 'to do's' is never-ending and Newfoundland weather is a fickle creature. Our major concern is whether or not Santa's helicopter will be cleared to fly.

This Saturday in December dawns sunny and bright, with a lovely coating of fresh, fluffy, white snow. It's 7:00 a.m., but Kelly Park is already buzzing with activity. Town maintenance personnel have cleared a landing pad for Santa's chopper on the ballfield, with 'Land Here!' carved in the snow so that it will be visible from the air. The caterers are in full-swing preparing for the hungry residents. Volunteers are setting tables and arranging children's activities.

And the countdown begins. When the doors to the community centre open at 9:00 a.m., we have exactly one hour until Santa's scheduled arrival time and it is controlled chaos as staff get everyone seated and through the buffet line. Despite the early rise and the tight seating arrangement, everyone is excited and the anticipation of Santa's arrival is palpable. Some families have been attending with their children for over a decade and are now bringing their grandchildren. For others, this is their first time attending with their own children. A whisper spreads: 'Santa's helicopter is good to fly. He'll be arriving from the North Pole very soon.'

Parents begin to get their children dressed to go outside and stake out the best possible spot to watch Santa's landing. Children are running and playing, parents are chatting and dishes are clanging when all of a sudden a shout goes up outside: 'I hear it!' and all activity stops. For a split second there isn't a sound inside the building or out as the children and adults strain their ears, eyes raised upward, listening for the first beats of the chopper blades.

From that moment forward the event erupts. The children are all clapping and cheering; even the most jaded of adults can't help but smile. The chopper flies directly overhead and then flies in long, slow loops around the field. There he is, Santa Claus, leaning precariously with one leg and one arm totally out into the open air waving at all the people below. As the helicopter slowly descends, it stirs up the fine, twinkling snow, temporarily obscuring the big man from view.

It's the real Santa from the Santa Claus Parade! The children swarm towards him and surround him in the snow. Some throw snow into the air creating a gentle mist as he leads them back into the warmth of the centre. Santa makes a snowball that he throws to one of the children and soon snow is flying and Santa is covered! He takes it all in stride and picks up a child and enters the building.

Santa has brought a small gift for each boy and girl, as well as his special teddy bear, which will be presented to one special child who has overcome insurmountable odds or who needs a little hope. The more extroverted children march right up to Santa, holding his hands and climbing on his back. Some children hold back, a little intimidated by the noise and activity. Santa will call those children to him, ever so gently, and pass them their gift and exchange a few words. Some of the younger ones simply stand and stare in awe, clutching their own stuffed animal.

Now Santa has spoken to every child and held every baby. The crowd stands in a large circle with Santa at its heart. It is time for the presentation of the special teddy. This year a little girl who is differently abled and *in a wheelchair will receive the bear. She is brought to the centre of the circle with Santa and the joy and pride she feels in this moment are evident by the huge smile that spreads across her face. This is her moment, presented to her in a magical setting by Santa Claus himself. There isn't a dry eye in the room amongst the adults as all the children cheer her on.*

Finally, Santa's time with the people of the Town of Logy Bay–Middle Cove–Outer Cove is done. As he prepares to depart, the children follow him as far as they are able, some calling out 'thank you' and others simply following along, swept up in the moment. The crowd reaches the safety barrier to the field; from here Santa must continue on alone as he makes his way to the helicopter. Every person at the event stands and cheers as Santa lifts off and waves goodbye until he is out of sight. Santa's presence with us has been short, but completely magical. Every person who attended leaves a little changed.

April

Chapter Nine

The Gathering Place

December 9th

" Santa, this is Sister Diane from the Gathering Place. Can you and St. Nicholas join us for our annual Christmas lunch?"

"Of course, Sister. We would be delighted to join you and your guests."

The Gathering Place is a welcoming, modern service centre in downtown St. John's. A joint project of the Congregation of the Sisters of the Presentation and the Sisters of Mercy, its mission is to build community, promote equality and provide nourishment. It exists "to meet the needs of people whom society has failed."

Many of their guests have complex issues ranging from physical illness and mental health problems to learning disabilities and addictions. They may live with abuse, or in poverty. They are male and female, young and old. They may be homeless. They certainly have needs that fall into the gaps of social programming. All are welcome as guests of the Gathering Place. It not only serves food to 150 people a day, but also provides many more services. There is foot and hair care, a clothing boutique and access to housing experts, nurses and social workers.

So just who are these Sisters of the Presentation and the Sisters of Mercy? Their presence in Newfoundland dates to Bishop Michael Anthony Fleming (1792-1850), who recruited two orders of religious women from his native Ireland to work as teachers. The Presentation Sisters, founded by Nano Nagle in Cork in 1775, established the Presentation Convent in St. John's in 1833, and the Sisters of Mercy, founded by Catherine McAuley in Dublin in 1831, followed in 1842.

"Hurry up, St. Nicholas. You are the patron saint of these guests so get into the sleigh and get on with your visit."

Santa's sleigh pulls up at the appointed time and he climbs out onto the pathway. Just inside the door, he is met by Mrs. Claus, a wonderful elf who has worked with him for years. We head down the long corridor, arm in arm, and music and dancing can be heard in the distance. For this special meal, all of the volunteers are invited and boxes of 'fast food' are generously donated as the kitchen team takes a well-earned rest. For many years, the meal was chicken and fries, and now it is burgers and fries. One year, as a guest was offered a box of food, he looked at it and said, "This is the first time anyone has ever given me my own meal like this. Normally, I only find what is left in garbage cans." Santa will never forget that comment.

Once the meal is finished, everyone assembles in a large central room. A local band is playing and the guests mingle with the clergy and the volunteers. Enter Santa and Mrs. Claus.

After the customary greetings, the elves divide the guests into male and female. Then, over the next half an hour, both Mr. and Mrs. Claus distribute large double-handled Christmas bags full of carefully selected gifts.

"What would the guests really appreciate on Christmas morning?" Santa and some Rotary elves had asked. "Soap, shampoo, tooth brushes and toothpaste, a warm T-shirt and weatherproof boots. A warm coat, hat and mitts or gloves."

Then the dancing starts. Santa looks around the room and sees a female guest standing alone, swaying to the music. Santa approaches her and invites her to dance. Luckily, it was a simple waltz and the elves had taught him the basics! Santa bowed to his dancing partner as the song concluded. She smiled back appreciatively and just as she turned, Santa took the teddy from his mail bag. Santa touched her arm and she looked back. "This is for you. Santa's bears are given to very special people and I will always remember dancing today with you." The guest was astonished and started to cry. She put her head on Santa's shoulder and sobbed. "In my whole life, no one has ever given me a teddy bear before. Thank you, Santa. I will never forget today."

Most of us bounce out of bed on Christmas Day to the sights and sounds of Christmas. The hot shower shakes the sleep from our bodies as we anticipate the gifts, the turkey and the trimmings. But for others, like the guests of the Gathering Place, the expectations are much more basic. Yes, a toothbrush, a facecloth and a fresh towel can make all the difference.

There is likely a facility somewhere near you, like the Gathering Place, that responds to "the needs of the people whom society has failed." Please assist St. Nicholas in your community and reach out to those in need.

CHAPTER TEN

THE DR. H. BLISS MURPHY CANCER CARE CENTRE

DECEMBER 10TH

In *The Night Before Christmas* Santa seemed to zip up and down chimneys, filling children's stockings and leaving their hoped-for presents with magical alacrity. He could do this because meticulous notes were kept in the North Pole of every child's wish, and because of global delivery organized with great precision across the world's Christmas Eves.

Now, my friend Santa sometimes gets to spend a little longer with a family, as there are four weeks between the Santa Claus Parade and Christmas Eve. So, there may be multiple opportunities to visit with a child. Once they see Santa in the parade and hanging from the helicopter, Santa owes it to the children to meet with them as often as he can. We have to keep the magic alive.

Let me share with you the story of Nathan, and how Santa got to see him several times.

In late November, Santa got an email from the CEO of the Dr. H. Bliss Murphy Cancer Care Centre. The building is attached to the Health Sciences Centre, the main hospital for the province. Also attached to this large building is the Janeway Children's Health and Rehabilitation Centre, usually simply called "the Janeway."

The email was to request a visit from Santa to see a very special little boy on a very important day in his life. This little guy, Nathan, had bravely gone into the hospital five days a week for six weeks, put on his "Star Wars" decorated helmet and lay in bed while the helmet was fixed firmly in place for his radiation treatments for a brain tumour.

The request was for Santa to be present at the conclusion of his 33rd treatment, which they would celebrate by ringing a bell, and for Santa to be the first person Nathan would see when he opened his eyes.

In March 2015, Nathan's family went on vacation to Florida. Nathan, his parents and grandparents planned to be there for a month. Almost as soon as they got there, Nathan started to throw-up every day. At first they thought it was stomach flu, or maybe an ear-related infection, as he is a good little swimmer. This went on for three weeks and was not much fun for anyone. In April, back in Newfoundland, more and more tests were done as his weight dropped by two or three pounds. Not good for a boy five-and-a-half years old.

Finally, in May, encouraged by Nathan's nanny (a retired nurse), it was decided to take a more aggressive approach towards a diagnosis, and a wonderful pediatrician said, "We will start at his head and work our way down but we will find out what is wrong."

Then, as Nathan's mother writes:

Nathan was diagnosed on May 20, 2015 with a brain tumour. At that time we didn't know the actual size, type or how long it had been there. That evening, we met our surgeon and he outlined what needed to happen.

May 27th, Nathan had surgery. It was one of the longest days of our lives. Everything went well. The tumour was fairly large, the size of a pear, and was then sent for biopsy. One thing a family thinks is: we never thought this would happen to us. But it did. We took it a day at a time, and still do.

44

As the tumour was attached to his brain, Nathan had some paralysis in his face. His eye was turned and he had to learn how to walk again. He was such a trooper! The biopsy came back and we were informed that Nathan had a rare tumour for a child his age, known as ependymoma. We knew that we had a journey ahead. We were discharged from the hospital on June 11th.

We returned to start chemotherapy on July 20th. He completed two cycles and finished them in September. Then, when he had another MRI [it showed] the tumour had returned and gotten larger. Where do we turn next?

October 5th we were sent to Halifax for a second surgery. The tumour, which was larger than [in] the MRI in September, was removed with a very small membrane left, as it was too dangerous to remove. The doctor indicated that he felt that he had removed 98 per cent of the tumour and membrane. They had done their best and they were pleased.

We came home on October 17th and the doctors said we had to do radiation as soon as possible. So that is what led us to the Dr. H. Bliss Murphy Cancer Care Clinic. November 2nd Nathan started radiation treatments and continued to do them each day for six weeks, giving him a total of thirty-three treatments without being sedated once! Some doctors didn't think he could do that but his mama did! During that time he had so much fun with all the technicians and a bond grew. He did not complain one day for his early rises to go to the clinic. December 17th Nathan rang the bell and it was another part of journey completed.

Just before the Santa Claus Parade, on November 29th, Nathan had approached Santa with his letter. An hour later,

Nathan looked up in the sky as Santa's helicopter arrived and landed for the parade. Santa waved to Nathan from the top of his sleigh, placed, as always, at the end of the parade.

And now, on December 17th, we all waited on the ground floor of the Dr. H. Bliss Murphy Centre. Nathan's final treatment was concluding only a few feet away, inside some very thick doors. Nathan's parents were present, along with a group of elves from Newfoundland Power who came with special gifts. (They do this for each child to celebrate the last treatment.) You could hear the sounds of some very big machines. Then things got quiet and finally a gowned doctor came from a side door and said, "You can go in now, Santa."

Santa reached in his mail bag. "Come on, St. Nicholas" said Santa. "We have a little boy to see."

The big door opened and Santa walked over to Nathan's bedside. They were releasing his head from the helmet; he was a little sleepy, but his eyes fluttered and he looked into 'the real' Santa's face, the one from the parade. Then his eyes got really wide and so did his smile. There were cheers from the whole staff, Nathan's family and the elves who had followed Santa into the treatment room. We had cupcakes, and this brave little boy sat quietly on the bed while a photographer recorded this wonderful occasion.

Then Santa turned and unzipped the mail bag. His teddy came out and went straight into Nathan's arms. Quietly, Santa left the room to allow the family to celebrate the ringing of the bell with their precious son.

Here is the post-script from Nathan's mother:

On Wednesday January 27, 2016, Nathan had a follow-up MRI to his radiation therapy. After a nerve-wracking few days we got results on Monday, February 1st, that the radiation was successful and there was nothing left! Needless to say, we're beyond happy!

We still know we have a long road ahead but it gives us a new starting point and a new baseline. MRIs will be every four months so if – and I mean if – it comes back, then we will have a better idea of the growing process.
Leanne

Chapter Eleven
The Kids Are All Heart
December 11th

Santa is well schooled in making his visits memorable for children. The first rule is to enter the room at the children's level; this may mean peeking in around a doorframe or crawling into a room on your hands and knees. In any case, you can't be above the children and looking down on them. You need to be a (big) kid, too!

One year, Santa was asked to visit a new group called the NL Heart Support Group, made up of parents and children; it is their children's congenital heart defects that they all have in common. The families have a unique, supportive bond and are really there for each other, answering questions and providing a shoulder to cry on.

This was a new adventure for Santa, visiting a group of children who may have had one, two or even three open heart surgeries. So, should Santa act differently? Are these children more fragile than those who do not have these challenges? Well, as Santa was about to learn, there are no differences at all! They are just as rough-and-tumble as any group.

Santa asked one of the mothers present for Santa's visit to tell you this story:

'Santa is here! Santa is here!'

Santa came into the gym and saw the kids' faces. The parents were astonished when he got down on the floor and crawled in. The kids surrounded him giggling and laughing. Then he put out his big, gloved hands and asked the children to help him get up, so they tugged and pulled him to his feet. He walked over to the mats on the gym floor holding hands with two of the children and there, once again, he lay down, opened his mail bag and took out a book. He showed them his pictures of the Santa Claus Parade and he even read a story to them. They were enthralled.

As he folded his book and put it back in the mail bag, he asked if anyone wanted a ride on his back and two brave little souls accepted his invitation and climbed on! The kids shouted with glee and cameras clicked, recording children as their parents had never seen them before.

Santa then got up and gave out some presents. Then, as he was getting ready to leave, he opened up his mail bag and pulled out a teddy bear. He wanted to give this extraordinary gift to our youngest little guest, whose name was Eric. He is a precious little boy who was enjoying the party; he was overjoyed to get this very thoughtful gift from Santa. His mom, dad and grandparents were filled with emotion at such a kind and caring gesture by Santa, especially because it was also Eric's first Christmas.

Santa waved goodbye and headed for the door and his flight back to the North Pole. Even after Santa left, the whole room talked about this remarkable visit and we were all still filled with emotion. To this day, when I ask Eric's mom about the special visit to her son, she smiles.
Krista

Chapter Twelve

Brighter Futures

December 12th

Santa does not always know what happens after his visits. In writing this diary of my Christmas adventures, I often gathered input from the event organizers, as they are the people in the room when Santa visits, and they feel the emotion and know what follows after the visits conclude.

"Hi Santa, I am calling from Brighter Futures. I have a big 'ask.' Can you do five visits to five chapters located widely over St. John's in the period of five days?"

Oh my! That is a big ask. Is all of that effort worth it? How does one decide?

The mandate of Brighter Futures is, "the healthy development and well-being of children and families within supportive communities. It provides the opportunity to talk to other parents about the triumphs and tribulations of parenting."

Brighter Futures is where, when Santa started visiting many years ago, a very young mother asked him to hold her infant while she went out for a cigarette. There were little red marks on the baby's face and Santa asked a support worker if the baby had measles. "No, Santa. That is the effects of OxyContin. Our mother is an addict, and we are helping her work through her challenges." It is also where, on a visit to the chapter in Marystown, Santa was reunited with his triplet friends – the first triplets that Santa had ever encountered, whom he had first met in the Janeway on Christmas Eve a year before.

Organizers of the visits sent me short accounts of what transpired after three of the visits to different chapters, and they varied widely:

One very important time of year for us is our annual visit from Santa. When Santa peeks around the corner there are bursts of laughter and the children scurry to see him. Parents' faces light up, too, for they are also living in this moment of utter glee.

Santa comes in and lies down on the floor, the children climb over him, look at photos and ask him questions. Parents look on and are consumed with their children's every move with Santa; for that moment in time all worries are forgotten.

Tucked into Santa's bag is a very special teddy. I recall a little girl a few years back receiving Santa's teddy. Katie talked for the rest of the year about that teddy, and how it was her most favourite gift. The magic Santa bestowed upon her heart that day will, no doubt, carry through her entire life. Imagine one simple act – but such a big impact.

A second visit was described in this way:

It is difficult to adequately describe Santa's visit to us in a few words. When Santa walks into the room, he takes us all along for an imaginary ride. Our hearts swell with compassion and Santa gives us a real gift that day. We are reconnected with that child-like anticipation and wonder of our youth, a feeling we share with our children. We believe once again. We carry this magical feeling in our hearts long after Santa has departed, for he had reawakened within us the true meaning of Christmas. In Santa's own words: 'It is our presence that matters, not the presents.'

And then this note came from a third chapter of this caring organization:

Hi Santa,

I don't know if you remember but you gave your teddy during your visit to the youngest child in the room.

His mom was suffering with postpartum depression and ended her life the first week of January. Your teddy and visit will be remembered forever. It is so tragic and sad.

I asked at the beginning of this chapter if the whole effort of visiting five groups in five days is worth it.

Santa and St. Nicholas meet the very young and the very old. We celebrate at every visit and try and spread cheer and reassurance. We can offer no assurance that all of the stories will end with "and they lived happily ever after."

All we can do is make the visits, try to spread the joy and pray.

SANTA'S MAIL BAG

Did you know that Santa was left-handed? Look next time you see him sitting high in his sleigh at the Downtown St. John's Santa Claus Parade with his mail bag draped over his right shoulder, across his chest and hanging on his left side. (You can also see Santa's teddy bear peeking out of the top and waving to all the boys and girls along the parade route.)

On all the visits that Santa makes, many children bring letters and they all go into Santa's mail bag to be delivered to the elves. Now let me tell you what else Santa might put into the bag.

The inside story:

Santa's big coat doesn't have any pockets, and some mornings he leaves home very early. On weekends, he could have as many as five or six visits over a period of five or six hours. This is because each visit lasts about forty-five minutes and then Santa has fifteen minutes to get to his next stop.

So, the first thing in the mail bag is keys to the sleigh or whatever transportation Santa is using that day. And, yes, Santa has his driver's licence in his wallet, just in case the local police ever need to stop him on his rounds. Next, Santa has a programmable GPS, which he and Mrs. Claus have loaded with street names and numbers the night before. You see, Santa must be on-time, often to the minute, as he has arranged with the event organizers to knock loudly on a front door at a very precise time.

During the Santa Claus Parade, Santa has his piece of the two-way communication equipment in his mail bag, as well. That is what he uses to talk with Mrs. Claus, who walks the whole route, about fifty yards in front of the sleigh. She is constantly in touch with Santa and giving him the names of children.

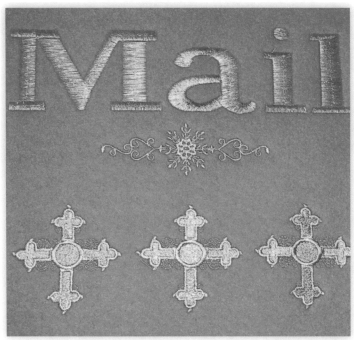

Yes, Santa carries a bottle of water in his mail bag, too. It is a long day with many strains and stresses on his vocal cords, and, just like any athlete, a sip of water is wonderful. Now, note I said a sip. It can be three or four hours from when Santa climbs up into his sleigh, fourteen feet off the ground, and when he can find the next washroom. So sips of water, that's all, Santa!

Santa carries a small camera as well, because Mrs. Claus often asks about his day. Santa can take pictures from the helicopter, or from the top of the sleigh, and he actually now knows how to take a 'selfie,' as the elves have shown him.

And, deep in the mail bag is a small stuffed replica of St. Nicholas. I travel everywhere with St. Nicholas and I find it very comforting. While it may sound peculiar, I often reach for St. Nicholas and ask that he go before me and prepare the way when I know that I have to go into the room of a dying child or a senior who is seriously ill. St. Nicholas is a critical part of my mail bag, and while he may be more than seventeen centuries old (the Santa we know today about 100 years old), his presence is very important.

Now, there are a few things about Santa's mail bag that you could not possibly have known!

Chapter Thirteen

Daybreak Parent Child Care Centre

December 13th

" 'Tis you, Santa. 'Tis you!" A little boy ran at Santa as he came through the door. My friend had heard the bells and was waiting for Santa to peek around the door, get down on his knees and crawl into the room. There are squeals of delight, a cascade of laughter and a look of awe and astonishment on many faces – child and adult. This little boy is from Newfoundland and is familiar with Santa, however, there are also many families here from different countries all around the world and this is not only new for the children, but new for the parents as well. They may never have seen Santa before. They may have different beliefs that don't include Christmas.

So, just where is this visit? Santa is at Daybreak Parent Child Centre in the east end of St. John's, Newfoundland, a community-based, not-for-profit association dedicated to children who are at risk, for different social or economic reasons. The amazing staff works to help them try to deal with issues like inadequate housing, poverty, food security and mental health, co-ordinating with other agencies that provide child protection. In addition, they assist a rapidly increasing number of people from other countries who have come to Canada wanting only the best for their children.

Santa wrapped his arms around the little boy who had greeted him with such enthusiasm at the door. "Merry Christmas, Jason," said Santa. "Mom, Mom, he knows it is me!" called Jason. "Of course he does," said his mother. "He is really Santa."

Outside, in the hallway, a staff member pushes a button on a little transmitter and whispers, "The little girl on your left is Hasmik. Her family has just come from Jordan." Santa turns to the child, who is standing hesitantly beside him, not quite sure what to do. "Hello, Hasmik. Welcome to Canada. I am Santa Claus and I hope you enjoy my visit here today." Her little brown eyes get very wide and so does her smile. Just behind her is her mother, dressed in a long black dress and a hijab. Two other young children are nestled against her and she holds a baby. This is a whole new experience for them, their very first Christmas in a new country. Who is this strange character in a red suit who is now opening his sack and taking out a book? He lies down on the mats on the floor and the children gather around. Santa starts to read, *'Twas the Night Before Christmas*, and the children are entranced. Santa asks if any child wants a ride on his back, and Jason is the first to jump at the opportunity. "Take off my hat and put it on your head," Santa says confidently. There is a gasp in the room from the staff as Jason whips off Santa's hat. Don't worry, Santa won't fall apart!

There is an opening in the crowd of children and Hasmik moves forward curiously. Her mother brings the little baby, who is placed in Santa's arms, and soon all five members of the family smile shyly in their very first picture ever taken with Santa.

Another parent tries to push a child forward to have a photo taken and the child resists. "You had better be good or Santa won't come to our house," the parent threatens. Ouch! Please don't blame Santa. A trained staff member takes the little boy's hand and together they approach Santa. The staff

member encourages the child. "It is OK to touch Santa. Can you feel the fur on his jacket?" Now the child feels calm and safe, and reaches carefully to touch something that he has only ever seen in pictures before: the fur trim on Santa's cuffs. He relaxes and smiles.

A few years ago, as the party was winding down, Santa looked at the staff as he unhooked his teddy bear from his mail bag. It was time for Santa to go, and, most of the time, his teddy bear stays with a child. As parents brought children to talk to Santa, a young girl was there who could not walk. Her name was Bridget and Santa gave her the bear. She wrapped her arms around teddy and someone whispered, "Good choice, Santa."

Over the years, Santa has learned many terms and acronyms and one is global developmental delay, a condition affecting children from birth to young adulthood. Because of the great effort from the team at Daybreak, Bridget can now walk and she and her family are progressing in dealing with the realities and her capabilities. It is in places like Daybreak, with the dedicated parents and staff, that this combination of early intervention and support makes a child's future more secure.

About five years ago, Santa's phone rang at his office. It was the project manager of an offshore mega-project and they had several hundred personnel in their office. Early in December, they had set up a large Christmas tree and all of the employees were invited to bring along a gift that would go to a needy family. The caller simply said, "Santa, you know where the greatest need is, so can I send over a few toys?" Of course, Santa agreed. Hours later, the door opened and fifty blue recycling bags came into Santa's office. They filled a corner 8 feet x 8 feet wide and 6 feet high. "There you go, Santa," said one of the drivers. "Deliver these to the children." There were only four or five more days until Christmas and Santa scratched his head. The hamper charities were all working to provide the food. Families in need had registered and, in some cases, other agencies had already met some of the ever-growing need. So Santa picked up the phone and called his elves at Daybreak. Within an hour, trucks were outside Santa's door and soon all of this enormous generosity was spread out for sorting at Daybreak. As well, a late call had come from a church saying that a family with ten children had nothing for Christmas. The elves got to work and soon this large family was provided for.

In another instance, the team became aware of a family from another country that had recently arrived and would be taken to a hotel until medical cards, permanent housing and immunization could be completed. What would Christmas be for them? What were their customs and traditions? These are very stressful times for many people and the staff at Daybreak responds as they become aware of those in need around them.

As he was about to leave, Santa reached out and shook hands with Jason. "Merry Christmas, my little friend. I hope you have a wonderful Christmas and I hope that you are standing right here next year when Santa comes back to visit!"

"You bet, Santa," said Jason. "I will be here for you."

Chapter Fourteen

The Murphy Centre Children's Christmas Party

December 14th

Santa's big sleigh pulls into the Murphy Centre and the parking lot is blocked with cars. This great facility was established in 1986 by the Christian Brothers as a response to youth whose educational needs were not being met in the regular school system. It was set up as a dynamic, alternative high school totally centred on the needs of its students. Santa knows that approximately 800 people avail of their services in academic, career and personal development/lifestyle training. Many of the students are young couples and young single parents. They know that their education is critical if they are to grow and provide for themselves and their families. And looking at the parking lot, it seems they are all here today with their children!

Santa is told that the participants have engaged in small fundraisers to help fund the event. It comes as a different feeling for Santa that the children are not just eager to see him. They are just as eager to see where their parents spend their day. It takes a lot of courage to make the decision to return to school– the children are proud of their moms and dads.

Just before Santa is due to arrive, the children gather for a song and dance party. Once the music stops they can barely contain their enthusiasm at the sound of Santa's sleigh bells! And of course, the traditional way to welcome the jolly old elf is with a rousing chorus of "Here Comes Santa Claus."

And with the hype at a feverish pitch, Santa comes through the door. Wading through a sea of children takes time and skill. The last thing Santa wants to do is to step on a small child's hand – no one wants that to be a memory for a child. So ever so gently, Santa slides forward. Then he gets down on his knees and asks the children to clear a little space so that he can lie down. Yes, lie down. For many years, Santa has watched parents take pictures from their height down on their child. Why not get down to the child's height and see the scene through the child's eyes? Slowly a space is cleared so that Santa can put his elbows on the floor and his hands under his beard. He starts to talk to the children and he asks them what questions they have. He reads them stories and he talks about the workshop at the North Pole. He entertains all questions and is generous with his attention, making sure no child goes unnoticed.

Then the moment that the children have waited for comes, when he asks if they want presents. There is a rousing cheer but Santa explains that he needs some help getting up off the floor, so the bedlam continues as children take his hands, arms and any part they can hold on to and pull Santa to his feet.

A small child takes Santa's big, white glove and leads him to the Christmas tree in the corner. Soon we start the distribution of the gifts and a wonderfully organized group of elves surround Santa, and they call the names of the children. The process must be followed efficiently because with fifty or sixty children, it takes time to get to them all.

After the gifts have been distributed, Santa can see parents reaching for boots and coats. But some of the children want to show Santa the gift that they have just unwrapped and that, too, is a magic time with the kids.

It is wonderful to ask a child how the new car operates, how the game is played or what secret powers the princess possesses. Pure magic unfolds when you talk to the children one on one.

As Santa is about to go back to his sleigh, a child comes forward with a package for him. He usually unwraps it with the children and they explain its use. While it is a memento of his visit, the children tell Santa that it is also something for his trip around the world. One year it was a keychain to keep track of the toyshop keys. Another year, a water bottle to keep him hydrated during his long journey. Then there was a tea cup to help wash down those delicious mounds of Christmas cookies! The children are sweet and considerate and they feel that it is important to show Santa their gratitude.

As Santa is departing, he is reminded of the thought expressed by one of the staff volunteers when he described Santa's visit to their centre. He said, "Ultimately the tradition of Santa and Christmas celebrations is about the dawning of new hope, a new beginning. The mandate of the Murphy Centre working with its students is just that as well – having the courage to begin again. Thank you, Santa. We all look forward to seeing you next year. Have a safe journey home."

CHAPTER FIFTEEN

THE CHILDREN'S REHABILITATION CENTRE

DECEMBER 15TH

Santa may be talented, but it takes a very large team to help him organize his pre-Christmas visits to the Janeway Children's Health and Rehabilitation Centre. Santa makes a number of visits to both the health and the rehabilitation departments of the hospital. On the rehabilitation side, Santa's elf Margaret T., or "Muggs," has been in the holiday picture for thirty-five years. Their biggest event is the breakfast at the RCMP building, which is held just before the beginning of the parade.

Imagine this scene with me. We synchronize our watches and are outside the door for our 10:30 a.m. visit. As we enter, met by two RCMP members in full-dress uniform, we can hear music and laughter, and, right on time, the band starts the song for Santa's entrance and we start down the long circular staircase.

Santa has learned a whole new vocabulary over the years, such as the term 'enabled differently.' That is certainly more positive and quite different from 'disabled.' Santa was also advised many years ago not to use the term 'handicapped,' which means 'less than.' The children may have autism, Down syndrome or another condition which keeps them in a wheelchair or frame. But they are shouting and waving, and other than the fact that some face pretty serious physical challenges this party is no different from any other.

As Santa comes down the stairs, some very familiar families greet him. Here he finds Chelsea and her sister,

Callie. Santa met Chelsea in the children's hospital many years ago on Christmas Eve when she awoke from a seizure, which had lasted for many hours, when Santa rang his bells. And there is Graysen and his whole family. Graysen is the first child Santa has ever met for two years in a row on Christmas Eve as a patient in the Janeway.

Physically and emotionally, a child's challenges can be very hard for many of their devoted parents, families and caregivers. This event is also a time to celebrate with the brothers and sisters and mothers and fathers. It happens before the parade because, while most of the children can be taken to the special section reserved for them, there are 60,000 people at the parade and sometimes the designated area is partially obstructed, no matter how hard we try to keep sightlines clear. It is very cold outside and the parade lasts about an hour with Santa at the end, so these children get their one-on-one time with Santa early, and Oh, what a special time it is. At about 11:30 a.m., Santa's elf signals. Santa takes the teddy bear from his mail bag and approaches

Graysen. There is a lot to celebrate today. Our little friend is breathing on his own.

Muggs shares her thoughts about just what happens on that special day:

Being part of Christmas at the Children's Rehabilitation Centre and the Janeway Children's Health and Rehabilitation Centre has left so many great memories, most happy but some sad.

Back in my early days at the rehab, the Downtown Parade was on a Saturday — a big outing for those patients who were able to go out to see it, while others waited patiently for them to return and tell them all about it. Santa came to visit the children after the parade and we would have pizza for lunch.

When the parade changed to Sunday, things got much bigger and we included staff and families in the event. So it evolved into Breakfast with Santa before the parade. The visit brings delight, joy, excited anticipation, and a certain status to these young children. After all, how many children have the 'real Santa' visit them on parade day?

The breakfast is an important tradition. The Turbot Cheeks, a band made up of the patient's dads and the staff play, our friends at McDonald's supply the food and the RCMP hosts us at B Division. What a fabulous way to kick off the Christmas season! It brings together so many people and is an opportunity for staff and their families to meet and celebrate with the rehab families. We sing our traditional songs, with the children dancing round, spinning in their wheelchairs, bursting with excitement, listening for the jingle of Santa's bells, and when they hear that sound, all eyes turn to the stairway and there he is, the Man in the Red Suit, on his first official visit of the season.

A parent once said to me, 'As great as the Janeway is, you can't always make our children better, but you can do what you can to make them happy.' We aim to do that all year round, and at Christmas, Santa and his teddy bears are part of making that possible. No matter who gets one of those bears, a memory is created for them all. Once a memory is made, photos, videos and sharing the experience with others, helps to keep it alive.

So many of the young people we see at the Janeway face unbelievable challenges, day after day after day. We do what we can to make them better, celebrating milestones and accomplishments to help create memories, including memories of a Janeway Christmas.
Muggs

Chapter Sixteen

The John Howard Society

December 16th

Santa and his colleague St. Nicholas have been visiting the John Howard Society in St. John's for more than fifteen years. It is one of Santa's favourite visits. The mission of the society is to provide "effective, just and humane responses to the causes and consequences of crime." It was established in Newfoundland in 1951, by a group of citizens concerned about the plight of prisoners and ex-inmates. It follows the mandate of the national organization to work toward penal reform and to create programs for the rehabilitation of offenders.

St. Nicholas has a special affinity and concern for this organization, as he is the patron saint of "the captives, repentant thieves, prisoners, the falsely accused and the unjustly condemned."

"Santa, this year's party is being held at an indoor climbing jungle and the children should have a wonderful time. If you come early, you can play on the bumper cars and climb the rock wall or Spider Mountain! Our event starts at 5 p.m. with pizza at 6 p.m. and your visit is set for 6:30 p.m. but you can come any time and join the fun."

Santa arrived at 6 p.m. and peeked in through the door. Children, secure in safety harnesses, were swinging from ropes suspended from the ceiling. Dry-land bumper boats with big, safe, inflated bows bounced around a fenced enclosure to the delight of the drivers. In the next room, children lined up to board a roller coaster-style swinging ride, where the pendulum swings back and forth, getting higher with each swing until it is eventually completely upside down and children are screaming in wonder. (I think Santa will take a pass, thank you. A four-foot inflated slide is about Santa's speed!)

The room is full of parents, staff and children. It is true that some of the parents are not here and are inmates, imprisoned locally or in federal institutions in other provinces. Here today, there may be others on parole, probation or temporary absence. But Santa can see that the children are having a wonderful time with their parents, who are enjoying the whole experience and just being kids themselves.

Soon boxes and boxes of pizza arrive and are delivered to the hungry partygoers. The elves beckon Santa to a big chair next to a very tall Christmas tree and the children gather. The John Howard Society staff are a well-organized team, and beautiful gifts are wrapped for every child. Each child's name is called and the gifts are delivered.

Then, an organizer nods to Santa as a shy little boy approaches. Santa recalls reading a book to this sweet child a short time before when he was there with his two sisters. Somewhere in the background, there were two adult females. Santa reaches into his mail bag and takes out his teddy. "Would you like to take my teddy to your house?" Santa asks the little boy. "Oh, Santa! I would love that. I will put him under the tree and tell my daddy when I am talking to him. He won't be home for Christmas."

Later, I am told all that I am allowed to know, which was simply that the children were there with their mother and a social worker, while under a restraining order with terms set by the court. This might indicate that the children are in child protection from one or both of the parents for some reason.

Santa waves goodbye and walks out into the snow. He was once told that the answer to overcoming an addiction is to "find something you love more." Maybe today, a parent held their child, laughed with Santa and felt the love and warmth that helped them take a critical step in a new direction.

CHAPTER SEVENTEEN

THE TUCKAMORE YOUTH TREATMENT CENTRE

DECEMBER 17TH

"Hi Santa, we are wondering if you can find the time in your schedule to visit the Tuckamore Youth Treatment Centre?"

This email arrived in Santa's inbox in late September and brought an immediate thrill and rush of emotion. This is what Santa knew about the Tuckamore Centre: It is a specialized place where they support youth with complex mental health issues. It was here that Santa had met one of his good friends again. Yes, Santa had seen this boy for many years at different social support agencies, and now as a patient at Tuckamore.

Some background:

For thirty-eight years Santa has had the privilege of visiting groups of children, and there are many organizations that ask Santa to return year after year. Through these visits, he gets to see children grow up, from infants to youngsters to teens. Some of the agencies are support groups that respond to the needs of parents, families and children. Between each association runs a connecting thread: poverty, mental illness, the criminal justice system, or health issues like heart problems or autism. (Of course, this is not always the case. There are many visits to children at parties, corporate events and parades.)

Sometimes, a child moves from one group to another and such is the case for Santa's friend at Tuckamore, whom

Santa first met through a group that works with offenders and their families.

The Tuckamore Youth Treatment Centre describes its role in brochures and websites as the following:

The name Tuckamore seems most appropriate for in Newfoundland it is the name we give to a tree that is growing, surviving and thriving despite living on the edge in the harsh coastline environment. This name reflects the resilience of the youth staying at the centre and their potential to overcome and flourish despite difficult challenges.

Over the past year, we have had eighteen youth come through our doors. They have been both male and female aged twelve to seventeen, hailing from all regions of the province. On average, they have stayed with us about four months and have come to us from varying socioeconomic and cultural backgrounds with a wide array of complex mental health issues. For example, a youth who required close supervision at all times upon admission because of high risk behaviours, is now able to go for bike rides, community outings and attend sporting events with only one staff. Another youth who came to us with self-destructive behaviours is now building therapeutic relationships with staff and taking pride in using healthier coping skills to deal with negative emotions.

I typed: "Yes, Santa would love to come to Tuckamore."

Now, join me now on the visit.

It is four o'clock and the parking lot is full. Many parents and friends are invited, for today is the centre's Christmas party and each member of the house is participating in a talent show. There are six youth residents and Santa is met at the door by one of the wonderful support staff. We wait for one of the acts to conclude and Santa enters the room. There is one youth for whom this is an especially difficult time. He knows Santa, as he and Santa have been buddies almost all of his life. He is not quite sure what to do when Santa walks in and he sits patiently in his chair, but Santa sees him and opens his arms. Our little friend jumps up and gives Santa a long, genuinely loving hug. Santa sits beside him as another youth is introduced and goes to the microphone. She reads a lovely poem and receives a standing ovation from her friends, staff and the other youth.

Now, Santa does have resources and had asked prior to his visit what the young residents might have on their Christmas lists. The professional staff could only give a gender and an age with a suggested item like a makeup set, "Star Wars" puzzle or some Montreal Canadiens hockey gear. Happily, Santa has arrived with a full sack that he opens in the centre of the floor. His helper elf can decipher the coded tags on the packages (gender and age is all that Santa can know) and she calls out the names of the recipients. The gifts are unwrapped with great appreciation. This is a big event for these young people. Many will be here over Christmas and this visit with Santa may be the only one that they have.

My little friend sits quietly on the floor glued to Santa's right leg. Finally, Santa has to go and it is very hard for us both. I reach for the teddy bear and take him out of the sack. Be careful, Santa. These are troubled youth and this may not be the place to pick favourites. So Santa goes over to the tree and places the bear on a branch. He starts to wave goodbye and tells the gathering that Santa's teddy bear should stay with all of them and they need not worry about Santa's return on Christmas Eve. He will be back.

As trust builds between the youth and their social workers, and day trips are earned and planned, Santa asks what might make a special treat. "Can Santa find hockey tickets for the AHL games at our local stadium?" Of course Santa can; just call.

The children are in good hands here. One hopes and prays that when their treatments are complete they will be strong and grow and prosper. It is Santa's fondest wish that when he comes to Tuckamore next year a whole new group will be there, or better still, that all is well with the youth in our province and no children will be there at all.

Chapter Eighteen

Richard Rogers and the Knights of

Columbus

December 18th

One day, Santa got a call from a certain Newfoundland and Labrador politician. "Hello, Santa. This is Gerry. I am calling to ask if you can come to a very special luncheon for many of the forgotten residents in our city."

Santa clicked onto his schedule to see if the date, time and location could fit into his day.

"Yes, Gerry. Santa would be happy to join you. Who is the luncheon for, how many will be there and what are the details?"

For the next few minutes, Santa listened, enthralled by Gerry's "ask."

My brother Richard likes to give back to the community and he has a big heart. So he has a Christmas dinner for those who are disadvantaged, and find themselves in a time of need. No one is turned away; the location can hold 250 people and we would really like Santa to be there to share the spirit of Christmas with our guests.

We all have a different definition and response to charity. For some, it may be the donation of money, and for others, it is to roll up your sleeves and get directly involved with a group you care for. In this case, Santa's friend Richard reaches out and welcomes those who may be mentally ill, homeless, poor, elderly or simply lonely. He finds his guests through the social agencies and shelters. All are welcome.

There is a beautiful meal, musical entertainment, and clowns and elves for the children. Taxis are hired for anyone who may need transportation and the facility is fully wheelchair accessible.

Once Richard sets out to do this, a big crew is needed, and it starts in his law office. His assistants, Dallas and Stephanie, add new files to their already busy office workload. This task is completely different from the usual legal challenges.

So, how do you shop for, prepare, cook, plate, serve and clean-up after a lunchtime meal for 250 people? Richard reaches out to another team who understands and supports this type of real charity, and this is where the Terra Nova Council 1452 of the Knights of Columbus joins the story. In St. John's, the Knights have a multipurpose building to serve their members and the community.

The Knights of Columbus were established by Father Michael Joseph McGivney, a Catholic priest who accomplished a lot in his thirty-eight short years. On March 29, 1882, while an assistant pastor at Saint Mary's Church in New Haven, Connecticut, Father McGivney brought a small group of parishioners into what was then, and remains today, a mutual aid society, providing financial assistance after a man's death to his widow and orphans. The organization has four goals, the first of which is charity, and currently has more than 1.8 million member families and 15,000 councils worldwide.

So, Richard and his team join the Knights of Columbus and their team. It takes days of preparation to acquire the turkeys, the vegetables and the trimmings. Mounds of potatoes and carrots are peeled by fifteen volunteers. Turkeys are stuffed and put in large ovens. Huge pots of bubbling gravy are stirred on the stoves. As the guests arrive in the decorated room, the band starts up and the serving team fills trolleys to whisk hot meals down narrow aisles.

At the appointed time, an elf comes for Santa. The big doors open and down we go to the main floor.

Santa is warmly greeted by the guests as he makes his way forward. Children come and high-five Santa and ask how Mrs. Claus and the elves are doing. There are frequent questions about whether Santa got their letter and what kind of cookies Santa might enjoy when he comes on Christmas Eve.

When the families come into the room, they are given numbered tickets and once the meal is completed, Richard and his team go to the microphone at the front of the room. First, every child receives a beautifully wrapped gift. Richard's elves have spent hours at this part alone. Then the ticket draws award prizes of huge hampers of food, baskets of biscuits and candy, and gift cards for supermarkets until every family has won something.

Santa spies a little girl in a bright red dress. Although her mother reassures her, she seems a little hesitant as Santa approaches, but once he crouches down to her level on the floor she starts to relax.

"Kelly, Santa has a special gift for a special guest here today. Here is Santa's own teddy bear and I am hoping that you will take him home and look after him forever. Would you do that?"

Kelly's face lights up. "Oh, Santa! I would love to have your bear and yes, I will look after him." A glance at her mother confirms that Santa has made a good choice. There are tears running down her cheeks.

Soon the event comes to a close. Outside a fleet of taxis is ready to take the families home. The band disconnects the cords and cables, and instruments are packed away. The clean-up crew is in full-swing and dishwashers and sanitizers pour clouds of steam into the kitchen, as hundreds of plates and cutlery come through the system. Tables are broken down and chairs are stacked and placed on rolling trolleys.

Santa turns and waves goodbye just as little Kelly heads out the door, snuggling teddy, and climbs into a waiting taxi. "Bye, Santa," she waves. "See you again next year!"

Richard and his office practise real charity. So do the Knights of Columbus. They all do their part to find out what their community needs, and volunteer to help.

THE INTERNATIONAL SANTA CLAUS
HALL OF FAME

In January 2015, my phone rang and an amazing Santa from the United States introduced himself. This Santa has appearances over 200 days a year and has stood on the top of his sleigh in the parades of some very large U.S. cities. He told me that a group of people had looked at my involvement with the St. John's Downtown Christmas Parade in Newfoundland and saw that through Rotary International, many thousand children in the world would receive the polio vaccine due to the donations raised by my Santa efforts. His message was simple: I was to be inducted into The International Santa Claus Hall of Fame (Class of 2014).

As they say in Newfoundland, I was gobstruck! The caller referred me to websites with information about the institution and the ceremonies, and there I learned that my wife and I would go to Albion, New York, in June and there I would meet more than 300 fellow Santas and Mrs. Clauses from all over the world.

What an adventure! There are some very dedicated people who work awfully hard at keeping the dream alive. The event is actually a big convention of Santas with the induction into the Hall of Fame held one evening. Some Santas are "real bearded Santas" and they have their own group; there is a Santa drill team comprised of military officers. There were many bright red vehicles with lettering and logos and supplier exhibitions featuring "everything Santa," right down to cufflinks.

There was lots of time to mingle, to listen and learn. I met some wonderful people and I made some surprising discoveries about what "professional Santas" have learned over the years. One of the subjects that I found most interesting was a discussion of risk management.

For some of my colleagues, Santa is a business. That is not the case for me: in my thirty-seven years assisting Santa, I have never been paid directly. (Sometimes money is paid to a charity in Santa's name and that funding has assisted with polio vaccination and other children's causes.)

But here are just a few of the things that other Santas need to be aware of. Most of the shopping centre Santas now have two small chairs on either side of Santa's big chair. The whole notion of sitting on Santa's lap is quickly disappearing and photographers working with Santa are told never to take a photo until he can see both of Santa's hands. Santa cannot be seen with his hand on a child. Of course, police screening is a given and many full-time Santas carry $5 million to $10 million in public liability insurance in case they are accused of some impropriety.

This was all news to me (although I did have to send my police screening in advance) but an indication of the world we live in. The etiquette and customs of Santa are changing and it is good to be aware of just how carefully one needs to prepare and act.

Before the presentation, we reviewed the "Santa Claus Oath" and we pledged our commitment to its high standards.

It was then that I began to realize just what an honour I was about to receive.

The International Santa Claus Hall of Fame has named only forty Santas since its inaugural class of 2010, with fourteen living Santas in 2015. I was to be one of them; I was then (and am now) the only living Canadian. And to the organizers' great credit, on the night of the big celebration, the Master of Ceremonies announced that there were two Canadians there, and so the whole room stood, and on the big screen they put up the words to "O Canada," and everyone sang. It was followed by just as stirring a rendition of "The Star-Spangled Banner."

And just who are these distinguished Santas? You would certainly know some of them. For example, we have all turned on a television and seen the classic black and white movie "Miracle on 34th Street." The English actor Edmund Gwenn, who played Kris Kringle, is an inductee. So is Mickey Rooney, who was Santa's voice in several stop-motion films, including "Santa Claus is Coming to Town." The commercial artist and illustrator Haddon Sandblom, who drew the Coca-Cola Santa in 1931 is an inductee; and there's at least one woman.

And you thought that this was just a jolly man in a red suit!

Chapter Nineteen

The Flight to the North Pole

December 19th

The Flight to the North Pole is one of the most magical events that any child could ever participate in. For the eighteen children who are selected, it will keep the dream of Christmas alive for many years to come.

During November, 99.1 Hits FM, a local radio station, runs a contest for its listeners. The prize offered each day, for eighteen days, is a seat on the Flight to the North Pole. On a cold December morning, the children will board the plane, fasten their seatbelts and prepare for take-off.

Most of the children are five to eight years old. They enter the contest by writing and submitting one question they would like to ask Santa if given the chance meet him in-person at the North Pole. The children are selected by the station, and the next morning, live on the radio, the number is dialed (after a discreet call to the home the day before) and the child is requested to come to the phone. Thousands of children are tuning in to hear if they have been chosen as the seats are filled one by one. (A parent accompanies the child on the flight.)

Now, the only other thing that Santa will tell you here is that he is sent the questions the afternoon before the flight and he and Mrs. Claus have the evening to think through how Santa should answer. Most of the questions are fun, however some are very tough.

Santa is at the North Pole (really a PAL hangar on the other side of the airport) when the children arrive at the airport at 5:30 a.m., and they are met by the staff from Provincial Airlines. As one team member describes it:

It is 5 a.m. and our team of elves prepare for the arrival of the chosen kids. No one has slept a wink, as this truly is our favourite day of the year. Weeks of preparation still don't prepare us for the flood of emotions we are about to experience. The first child shows up at 5:20 a.m. and it is now reality. It's my fifth year as Chief Elf but for some elves it is their first year. As I watch them interact with the kids I get this overwhelming sense of joy.

The kids are so sleepy and it takes them a few minutes to grasp each step of what's actually happening as we go through security and board the flight. What's so magical about this day is, not only does it renew the children's sense of faith, but in some way, for every adult witnessing it in the airport, for every volunteer and staff member, maybe the audience hearing it on the radio, the ones who join us in Christmas carols after the flight, there's no other word to describe this day every year other than magical.

Debbie

Chief Elf - Provincial Airlines

The plane takes off, lands and taxis over to Santa's hangar. Santa lies on the floor and the elves cover him in real snow and he walks up the stairs and onto the plane.

Here, I would like to turn the story over to the mother of a little girl named Olivia, who was seated in Row 3. This beautiful little child, with her cherub face and movie star personality, is one of the estimated 120 people in the world with a disorder called Pearson syndrome. There are many complications. Her bone marrow and kidneys are just two of the parts of her body that are affected. She has diabetes, is nourished through

a feeding tube and sometimes has trouble walking. While she may know that something is wrong, don't tell her she is sick. She has a gorgeous presence and time stood still for us all when she hugged Santa on the plane.

It was another crazy day running here and there getting ready for Christmas and the phone rang. It was the school: 'Olivia is sick again; you'll have to pick her up.' I was about to leave when the phone rang again and the voice said, 'This is 99.1 Hits FM radio,' and on that note I knew my day was about to get a whole lot better. This was the call we were waiting for every single morning, and finally we got it. The call came for the Flight to the North Pole. I think I cried and I'm sure they thought I was unstable, but this was a dream actually coming true for one very special little girl.

A few weeks earlier Olivia and I had sat down and filled out an application to win a seat on the Flight to the North Pole. Going through the application I remember asking Olivia, 'What would you like to ask Santa?' Her innocent little voice said, 'Can Santa fix sick little girls and boys?' I lost it, as Olivia is very sick but has no idea how sick. I said to her, 'Maybe you would like to ask Santa something else?' She said, 'No.' So we left it at that. Every morning she would sit next to the radio waiting to hear the call.

Olivia was over the moon excited that she was going to meet Santa the very next day. She continued on to school and told everyone in her path that she had won the bonus seat on the Flight to the North Pole.

That evening we decided it was best for us to stay in a hotel closer to the airport because of Olivia's medicine regime and the 6 a.m. arrival time at the airport for departure. So off we went to the hotel for the evening. She was so excited it was hard to get her settled, she had so many questions as to what was going to happen. She wanted us to wear our snowsuits as the North Pole was freezing, and finally she dozed off still babbling about how she was going to finally get to meet the real Santa!

Four a.m. came early and Olivia woke feeling very sick and throwing-up. I thought right away we weren't going to get to go, but she came around and we made it right on-time, with a few minutes to spare, after she had a hot cup of tea and a tea bun. I managed to talk her out of wearing the snowsuits, as I told her that Santa was magical and we wouldn't get cold, so we only needed gloves. When we entered the airport, she lit up like a Christmas tree when she saw all of Santa's helpers buzzing about and all the other children that were going to meet Santa, too. We mingled and chatted with all the other excited moms and kids and the announcement came to get our boarding passes. Olivia was one of the first in line as small as she is, and as proud as a peacock, she accepted her pass and said, 'We are really going to see Santa, Mom, we are really going!' As everyone made their way to security her smile alone brought a few tears. This was one of her dreams come true and I got to be part of it.

As we got to the gate and finally heard the call to board the plane – well, I thought she was going to lose it and if she wasn't, I was! Then the countdown: three, two, one, takeoff! It was real and she was buzzing with happiness, everyone was. All the windows were wrapped so no one could see where we were flying, as Santa's North Pole is a secret and not everyone gets to go. In no time flat, we were landing. When she saw the red light through the paper-wrapped windows, she knew it was Rudolph. Soon we could all hear the reindeer on the top of the plane and she grabbed me just as they announced Santa was coming on board, as it was too cold to get off. She just froze with excitement.

Santa boarded the plane, walked up the aisle and shook the snow off his suit. Some landed on Olivia's hand. As Santa was busy and had so much to do, he got right to work talking to all the boys and girls about their questions they had for him. While Santa was doing that, his elves were delivering gifts to each child on the plane. Olivia opened her gift only to be totally surprised: Shopkins. How did Santa know, because she never had it on her list. He was in her good books for sure. Santa finished giving his presents but he had one special little one left, his very own teddy bear. He would choose one child to take his bear home and look after him forever. Olivia was to be that child. Santa gave her the bear, picked her up and put his hat on her head. He gave her a hug she will never forget in her lifetime. Santa led Olivia back to her seat where she guarded her bear for dear life. He had to go *and get back to work and we had to return home, so with a 'Merry Christmas' and a 'goodbye,' Santa was gone.*

We took off and got instructions that we could unwrap the windows to see where we were, and because of Santa's magic we were over St. John's in warp speed. We sang songs again all the way home. As we were landing, Olivia looked at me and said, 'I can't believe it, I got to meet Santa and I got his teddy bear. I can't wait to tell everyone.' We entered the airport to music, food and friends – everyone celebrating an event that only a select few could truly appreciate, and we truly appreciated every minute of it.

Colleen

Olivia's question was the toughest of the eighteen questions that Santa was asked to answer that day.

"Can Santa fix sick little girls and boys?"

So, how did Santa answer her? He gave her a big hug, put his hat on her head, looked into her eyes and then he said, "No, Olivia, Santa can't fix sick little girls and boys but Santa does have an amazing group of doctor and nurse elves at the Janeway Hospital and they do their best every day to fix sick little girls and boys. You are in good hands."

She slowly released her tight grip around Santa's neck, took the bear and snuggled next to her mother in her seat.

Chapter Twenty

The Contrasts

December 20th

Santa makes many visits to the Janeway Children's Health and Rehabilitation Centre in St. John's: The Janeway, as it's widely known, is the children's hospital. The first visit, usually in the first week of December, is for the photo shoot with the babies in the Neonatal Intensive Care Unit (NICU) and the nursery. We may head over to the Pediatric Intensive Care Unit (PICU), as well, but it all depends upon the number of children in each area.

Santa arrives at 2 p.m., usually on a Tuesday, with a teddy bear peeking out of his mail bag and tightly held in place. Velcro is great stuff. When we get off on the third floor, Santa is met by a team leader and taken to the Christmas tree and rocking chair arranged in the hallway. The hospital photographer is on hand and the names on the very small arm bracelets are checked off on a clipboard. The little ones have been carefully dressed in some very cute festive outfits. Blankets hide IV tubes and oxygen cylinders so that the whole scene appears as normal as possible. There are usually several sets of twins, and one year we even held triplets.

The photo shoot lasts about an hour, with between thirty and forty newborns brought and placed in Santa's arms. The gentle sound of the sleigh bells and the rhythm of the rocking chair seem to calm the occasional fussy child who has decided that now is the time to exercise his or her lungs, so that baby's first Christmas photo can be taken and given to the parents.

When all of the children who can be brought to the tree to meet Santa have been photographed, Santa is asked to come into the NICU. Here we meet the really tiny newborns, some only a few hours old and weighing less than 600 grams (just over 1 lb). These very little children are in special medical cribs where heat, light and moisture are constantly monitored and controlled. They are too small and too fragile to be moved so Santa gets down behind the side of the crib and the photographer captures the image through the clear plastic. In most cases, there are anxious, distressed postpartum mothers sitting vigil, hoping against all hope that their child will respond to the very best efforts of the professional staff. Santa knows from his years doing this that he will likely receive a nod from a head nurse or doctor that Santa's teddy should stay with a particular child. I don't ask questions, as I am not allowed, and I fully support the rules of hospital privacy.

On one occasion, Santa reached into his mail bag and released the little straps. Then he looked to the mother and said, "Santa has very special teddy bears. Look, the little scarf says 'Santa's Own Teddy' and my teddy bear usually stays with a very special child who Santa knows will give him a warm and loving home. Would you accept Santa's teddy for your child, and all of the blessings which come with your child?"

At the sound of Santa's voice, the child's mother looked up, but she was too upset to say a word, and she put her head down and let the tears drip into the tissues she was holding.

That was Santa's last visit in the unit and, at 4.30 p.m., Santa left the hospital.

Later that week, on Thursday morning, the minister of our church, St. Andrew's, called to say that an elderly member of the congregation had passed away. He told me that the funeral would be the following Monday and that the wake was being held at a funeral home not far from the church. I began organizing the service by arranging for ushers, parking attendants, funeral brochures, etc.

I looked at the obituary and found the visitation hours. I went to the funeral home at 2 p.m. on Friday and I noticed that the parking lot was full. As I went through the main doors, there were many young couples and I looked up at the notice board to see what room what being used for our elderly church member. She was resting in Room 6. I started down the hall with that nervous feeling of not wanting to look in the other rooms.

When I got to Room 3, I could hear that someone was upset. I turned my head and in the room was a small, white, open coffin. On the left side of the coffin was a single yellow rose and on the right side was Santa's teddy bear.

Oh, St. Nicholas. How do I behave? I went into the room of complete strangers. The mother, surrounded by her family and friends, was weeping and holding the baby. People deal with grief in different ways and we cannot be judgemental. From my wallet, I took my Santa Claus driver's license, with the photo of Santa. I showed it to the mother, who stood and said, "We will never forget Santa's time with us in the hospital and his teddy will be a part of our lives forever."

Thank you, St. Nicholas, for giving me the courage and the strength to go into that room. I just knew that it was the right thing to do, and I knew that St. Nicholas had gone into the room first and was there for me when I slowly walked in.

CHAPTER TWENTY-ONE

GRAYSEN

DECEMBER 21ST

Graysen and his family have been with Santa for the first three years of Graysen's life. Santa met him with his mother, Alice, in PICU on Christmas Eve when he was one-year-old. Then, to Santa's great surprise, we met again in the same place on the same night when Graysen was two. In the thirty-seven years of Santa visits, we had never met the same child twice on Christmas Eve in the Intensive Care Unit. So, Santa's teddy went to Graysen.

Graysen's challenges continued and, the year after that, Santa met him outside the hospital at a children's party held at RCMP headquarters by the Children's Rehabilitation Centre before the parade. Santa did not know that Graysen and his family would be there and it was a great thrill to walk into the room, look over in the corner and see his wonderful little friend, cradled in his mother's arms. It seemed appropriate that this little trooper should have another bear.

But here is Alice to tell us herself what it was like to be there with her son when Santa walked down the winding staircase and the band was leading a chorus of "Here Comes Santa Claus":

Picture this, December 24, 2013. Our second Christmas in a row at the Janeway with our son Graysen. Although, oddly enough, this year there wasn't half as much anxiety as the year before. Why, you ask? Because Santa is coming!

Photo credit Kim Hart

Graysen was the only child in PICU that year. That in itself was a little harder to deal with. Other children were sent home days before Christmas. Home where they belonged. But we had to stay. Not that our friends at the Janeway wouldn't have loved to be able to send us home for Christmas. It just wasn't in our immediate future.

Graysen was born with Cornelia de Lange syndrome, but on top of this was diagnosed with chronic lung disease, and at this particular time he was on a high flow of oxygen to help keep his lungs open. As we were unable to sit around our own Christmas tree at home, our friends brought the tree to Graysen's bedside. We sat there in silence as we took in the glow from the tiny lights. Then the sound I had been waiting to hear echoed through the hallway: Santa's bells!

Santa came and, remembering us from PICU last year, stayed and visited for a little while. Before he left he reached in his sack and pulled out a teddy bear. Not just any old teddy bear, but Santa's Own Bear. You see, there is a huge difference between your typical teddy bear and Santa's Own Bear. The typical bear is woven with thread, filled with fluff and covered in fur. Santa's bear is woven with love, filled with hope and covered in trust. And not just any child gets the honour of receiving this treasure: only the strongest children facing some of the hardest battles. As he was handing me this teddy bear all I could do was cry. I was so honoured, as my son Graysen has battled many a demon. He is my hero and always will be, but knowing that others see him in the same way ... there are no real words to describe this happiness. I'm pretty sure I was glowing brighter than the tree.

The following year, we managed to get home for Christmas. Only barely, might I add; the 22nd of December, 2014, we were discharged. We had the most amazing Christmas at home. Which brings us up to the November 2015 Christmas party. I wondered if Santa would remember us, as it had been two years since he had last seen Graysen. All the kids were lining up to get to sit on Santa's knee. But even with all the commotion, Santa spotted us in the crowd and came over, picked up our little boy and sang and talked to him.

Watching Santa with Graysen was beyond emotional. This little boy, who has been through so much and still faced a rough road, was now just a little boy in Santa's arms. Right where he should be: at a Christmas party, instead of in a hospital. We talked for some time about how well Graysen has been doing, how he's been able to come off of the daytime oxygen. What a miracle he is. All these positive things. Then, before passing Graysen back, Santa once again stuffed his hand down in his sack and pulled out the bear! He gave it to Graysen; then, giving me a hug, he said, 'I will always remember.'

It's not enough to say that being given a teddy bear from Santa is an honour. It is so much more than that. It brings so much joy, so much hope, not just to the child who receives it but for the family, as well. These teddy bears mean more to me than they could ever possibly mean to Graysen, as they came at a time of great need for joy and hope. When all else seemed lost, these little bears helped to remind me that although things seemed overpowering, there is a light at the end of this dark tunnel.

Graysen, like any other three-year-old, has quite the collection of stuffed toys and animals. We have everything from bees to dragons, puffins to turtles. They all have their own special story as to how they came to be displayed along Graysen's shelf, but no story will ever be told as often as the story of Santa's Own Bears.
Alice

CHAPTER TWENTY-TWO

"FOOLED YOU, SANTA!"

DECEMBER 22ND

Santa parked his sleigh outside the three-storey senior's home and looked toward it through the swirling snow. He checked his watch to confirm that he was five minutes early and he closed his eyes briefly and thought about the visit he was about to have. This was the fourth that day.

Senior's homes can be both happy and sad places to visit. There are many people who are bright, happy and full of life. Then, in the next room, one can find a small mound under a blanket. The lights are dim, their breathing is shallow and their eyes can stare off with no recognition that Santa is in the room and gently ringing his bells. This is the building where one resident, in answer to Santa's question, "What would you like for Christmas?" said in a very sad and haunting voice, "Tell my children where I am on Christmas Day and tell them that I miss them and I love them."

So what will Santa find today? We have been coming to this building for more than twenty years and have seen some very beautiful people pass through. There is an amazing, caring staff and all of the residents feel their respect and support.

With a hearty, "Ho, Ho, Ho!" Santa proceeded up the driveway, through the big double doors and into the reception area. There he met his elves, all appropriately dressed, and on schedule to arrive in the children's daycare in the basement in two hours' time.

This is another building where there are different levels of care. On the third floor, many of the residents are able to walk and can find their own way to the dining room and the large, comfortable lounge areas. Then, as one descends from floor three to floor two, and finally to the first floor, personal and nursing support increase to meet the needs of each resident.

Santa got off the elevator on the third floor, and followed his elves down the long corridor. At the far end of the hall, an elderly woman leaned into her walker and moved toward us with purposeful, strong strides. Her walker had Christmas green trim and lights. She pushed a button on one of the handles and suddenly "Santa Claus is Coming to Town" played for us all to hear. She was dressed all in red and had a clip of holly in her wavy grey hair. Rudolph's bright red nose blinked on her handlebars.

"Hi, Santa," she called in a strong voice. "Welcome back. I brought something to show you." As she approached, she reached down into a bright, velour bag and pulled out a teddy bear! It was one of Santa's bears from the year before! "Look, Santa, you gave me this last year for my 100th birthday. Fooled you, didn't I! You didn't expect me to be around this year did you?"

Santa let out a hearty laugh and asked her the secret of her good health. She told me that she had never smoked, exercised every day and regularly enjoyed a glass of sherry at 4:30 p.m.

But it was her next statement that caught Santa off guard. As this dear soul, eyes twinkling, stood in front of me, I leaned forward and quietly asked, "And what could Santa bring you for Christmas?"

Without any hesitation, she leaned forward and tugged on Santa's beard. She pulled him forward and whispered loudly in Santa's ear, "Go to bed with me, Santa. Go to bed with me!" My elves erupted into laughter and my friend wheeled her walker and scurried down the hall[1]. Finally she turned and called, "If I make it to 105, do I get another bear?"

Santa makes no promises. He has to get there, too!

Santa recovered his composure and we trooped down the hall.

Next we entered the happy room of an eighty-five-year-old gentleman who was a very well-known local broadcaster in his day. He had a great personality, a wonderful outlook on life and he spread cheer and good wishes wherever he went. He was a joy to be with and loved by the other residents on the floor.

Santa swept into his room with a hearty, "Ho, Ho, Ho!" Once we had exchanged greetings and told a few stories, Santa said that he had a question that perhaps his guest could answer, as he had been the host on many "Open Line" shows.

"Fire Away, Santa. What can I help you with?"

Santa said discreetly that he had encountered a lady in the building who had asked to go to bed with Santa! (Naturally, no names or locations were discussed, and once again, my three staff members were Santa's witnesses.)

My aging friend thought for a minute, and he looked up and said, "Lend me your hat, Santa. What is her room number?"

[1] Santa tries very hard to have witnesses whenever he is with vulnerable adults or children. Police screening is not enough so I have staff witnesses who can attest to this dear lady's response to my question.

Santa is still laughing even as the author types this story. Santa was so impressed that he reached into his mail bag and took out the teddy. He explained that on every visit, Santa's teddy stayed with a very special person, and he asked if this wonderful man would find a good home for the bear.

An hour later, having visited the daycare and read to the children, Santa left the building, chuckling, and climbed into the sleigh.

In the North Pole that night, he regaled Mrs. Claus and all the elves with the story of his visit to the seniors' home.

THE KNIGHTS OF ST. NICHOLAS

In 2016, the author was asked to attend a service in Branson, Missouri, where he would go through a solemn ceremony. He would kneel on the floor and a sword would be used to make him one of the very few members in the world of the Knights of St. Nicholas. Each of the recipients receives a blessing with holy water mixed with the sweet-smelling manna of St. Nicholas, believed to emanate from the relics of St. Nicholas entombed in his Basilica in Bari, Italy. The liquid is blessed during a church mass held prior to the anointing. The inductees are expected to uphold a "higher calling than the Santa Claus experience." While neither a Catholic nor Protestant effort, the Knights of St. Nicholas promise to "to keep Christ in Christmas."

One is not made a knight without a vigorous process of references and checks. But in addition to all of that, there is a commitment to uphold:

The Creed of the Knights of St. Nicholas

I believe in the miracle of the manger and the message of the child who was born as the Messiah as God's true gift to all mankind. I acknowledge the Passion and the sacrifice made as a paradigm that it is truly better to give than to receive.

I understand the devotion of Nicholas of Myra and his conviction to God's love for all mankind as an example to follow. I am a mere mortal who has no magical powers except the belief of loyalty to the tradition of the Advent Season that has been handed down from generation to generation to me by my family and friends.

I acknowledge that the true basis for the celebration is the child of the manger and I promise to make all children happy to the best of my abilities in his name. I confirm

these beliefs to myself and to the Spirit of Christmas as a Knight of St. Nicholas, a servant of people everywhere.[1]

In a number of chapters in this book, I have repeated that in Santa's mail bag, there is a St. Nicholas, and on more than one occasion, Santa reaches into his mail bag to hold and receive the reassurance of St. Nicholas. Not all of the visits are easy. Not all of the children survive in the hospital and some of the elderly may be in their final days and hours of life.

I do believe that children need to be told about St. Nicholas, and not just Santa. Just as it is important to remind children that Clement Moore's *The Night Before Christmas* is actually titled *A Visit From St. Nicholas*, and Santa is not mentioned once.

The story of St. Nicholas goes back seventeen centuries to a town called Patara, Lycia, on the southern coast of what is now Turkey. As a young man, Nicholas had a love for Jesus and that led him to follow in an uncle's footsteps and become a priest.

[1] "The Creed of the Knights of St. Nicholas," "The Santa Claus Creed," "Santa's Creed," and other connotations are copyrighted under an attachment with Arcadia Publishing 2010 by Phillip L. Wenz. ISBN # 978-0-7385-4149-5 and LCCC # 2007925452 - All rights reserved.

After his parents died in an epidemic, Nicholas received a "good amount of money and property" and he was able to choose how he wanted to spend it. Nicholas was chosen to be the Bishop of Myra, and it was in that role that he was able to do so much for others.

There are many legends of Nicholas: how he fed the people following a famine; how he threw coins through the window of a poor widower with three daughters and they landed in a stocking; how he climbed onto the roof of a home where there was great poverty and he dropped a bag of gold coins down the chimney so that no one could see him leaving gifts outside the family home. As you can see, these early acts have defined our traditions.

In 325 AD, Bishop Nicholas attended the Council of Nicaea, the site of some very great decisions, like the Nicene Creed, which still informs and structures Christian beliefs. Nicholas died on December 6th, what is now St. Nicholas Day, in 343 AD.

While being Canada's only living inductee of the International Santa Claus of Fame is a privilege, membership in the Knights of St. Nicholas brings both opportunities and a higher bar of responsibility, as we work, visit by visit, not just to keep the magic of Christmas alive for children, but also to uphold the ministry of St. Nicholas.

CHAPTER TWENTY-THREE

CHRISTMAS EVE AT THE JANEWAY: MICHELE

DECEMBER 23RD

Christmas Eve about 8 p.m., my daughter Dr. Christina Templeton and I arrive in the parking lot of the Janeway Children's Health and Rehabilitation Centre. Out of the trunk comes a big suitcase and we pull it along, sometimes through the snow, into the entrance of the hospital. Once in the building, one realizes just how quiet it is. There is a mural of animals and the familiar Christmas tree in the stairwell-area but sometimes we have taken that long walk toward the elevators and have not met anyone at all. If Santa had one wish on Christmas Eve, it would be that there would be no children here, either. But that has never been the case in over thirty years of these visits, so we continue on to the third floor where there is a small meeting room near the offices of the pediatric doctors. I close the door and twenty minutes later Santa is ready to start on his Christmas rounds with his Chief Elf, Dr. Christina.

Who will we meet on our Christmas rounds, Santa's last visit for the year, as we travel through Surgery, the wards, PICU, NICU and Emergency?

One thing that stands out, as we travel from floor to floor, department to department, is the staff. They are absolutely dedicated to their patients and they do their utmost on this night to keep the spirit of Christmas alive and well.

On our first visit to the surgery floor, a teenager is lying on an elevated bed; his foot has been bandaged. He has earphones on and is bobbing to the music, as his fingers and thumbs race across a game controller and a space game engrosses his attention on a screen. "Hi, Santa," he says, slipping the headphones down around his neck. "Thank you for coming to see me." All that Santa knows at this point is that his name is Greg, because that is written on a clipboard at the end of the bed. "Merry Christmas, Greg," Santa responds. "What brings you in here on Christmas Eve?" "Santa, I did something stupid. I shot myself when I was cleaning my father's gun." Another first for Santa. "Can you bring me the new hunting video game for Christmas?" our young patient asks. "I will do my best, Greg," and we wave as we leave the unit.

Every Christmas Eve brings its challenges and it is important that Santa see every child. Soon we come to an isolation unit and the nurses are ready for Santa at the central station. "We are going to gown you, Santa. Hold out your arms." Santa's big gloves slide through the yellow gown and the strings are attached. Santa gets his instructions. "Don't be too long, Santa. Don't leave anything in the room. The child is very prone to infection. You are going in alone as there can only be one person in the room with the child. Cover your gloves in the disinfectant." Big brown eyes open wide and a little face smiles as Santa's bells gently bring a little girl from a drowsy sleep. "You came, Santa. You came. Mommy said that you would find me."

At about 9 p.m. we reach NICU and here we meet some very new and often very small children. All around the children and parents, the monitors blink and beep. Santa moves from rocking chair to rocking chair and, if at all possible, every baby is lifted from a tiny bed and placed in Santa's arms. Many of them have the cutest hats and festive blankets. Parents watch as photos are taken and often there is a family picture done, as well.

One year, Santa met the newest child in the unit; he had been born at noon. The baby was there with his dad, as apparently his birth had taken some time and his mom was resting. As they took this 12 lb. boy from his crib, the nurses announced that he was the biggest child in the unit. Then Santa chuckled at the child's outfit designed in a familiar red, white and blue pattern. "Turn him around, Santa," said the dad. The little guy was decked out in a Montreal Canadiens uniform with "Go, Habs, Go" on the back. "Never too young, Santa. Got to teach them early!"

Each year, before we leave this unit, we usually ask if any of the nursing staff have children at home. There are always one or two and soon we hear, "Hi kids, this is Mommy. Guess who is here at work with me in the hospital?" Santa rings his bells into the phone. Sometimes, we talk to the children, as well, and suggest that they go straight to bed because Santa is coming down their street very soon. Magic, pure joyous magic.

Before we leave the hospital to get back to the North Pole, we are asked to go into a room where a family is present and a special patient, Michele, is asleep. Michele's mother, Janice, tells us what happened next:

Michele was born with Down syndrome and she seemed to be battling something her whole life. At six months old, she had open heart surgery to repair a hole in her heart and her valves were joined together. Also, she had tubes placed in her ears and her eyes needed to be straightened. She didn't walk until she was five and it was then that her sister was born. It is a challenge to bring up children where one may have special needs but it

Photo credit C. Templeton

is important to treat them the same. Michele had to learn that she got no special treatment.

In September 2001, when she was twenty, she was diagnosed with leukemia and, through a special study of patients up to twenty-one, she became a patient of one of the best oncologists Newfoundland has ever had, Dr. Jack Hand with the Janeway.   She went through extensive treatment over many years. Finally, the disease went into remission. Then, in July of 2007, her cancer returned and she got weaker into the fall.

In 2011, Jack Hand was diagnosed himself and he would tell the children that he understood how they felt and that he was going through the same thing. Dr. Hand died of a brain tumour on June 6, 2012.

Michele loved Christmas and Santa. She said that Santa was her great friend and she adored him. On December 21st, a Monday, her condition worsened and *she had to be admitted. On Thursday, December 24th, Christmas Eve, she lay in the bed and did not wake up at all. The nurses came and took her vitals but she did not move. At 9 p.m., my mother, brother and sister-in-law came in. They had all the gifts and we made plans for Christmas Day. Then we heard the bells and the nurses said, 'Santa is here and he will be with Michele shortly.' Soon Santa came into the room and he went over beside her. The nurses raised the head of the bed and Santa put his arm around her. For the first time that day, she opened her eyes. She whispered, 'Santa, Santa,' and she snuggled into his arm. Pictures were taken and I felt a great sense of joy, for I knew that she was aware that Santa was with her. Santa meant so much to her and I knew that she was at peace. She closed her eyes and went back to sleep.*

At 3 a.m. on Christmas morning, the nurses checked her vital signs and about 3:15 a.m., she passed away. She was surrounded by love and by bears. Some children in a Labrador school had sent beautiful bears to the children in the hospital and one was there with Michele. And her own Pooh Bear was there, too. Her bear was buried with her.

She will be in our hearts forever and a second Labrador bear sits on the keyboard in our house as a daily reminder of the beautiful daughter who died on Christmas Day and whose last words were 'Santa, Santa.'

Janice

CHAPTER TWENTY-FOUR

CHRISTMAS AT THE JANEWAY: CHARLIE

DECEMBER 24TH

One Christmas Eve Santa met Charlie, one of the cutest little people Santa has ever seen.

In order for Santa and his Chief Elf, Dr. Christina, to see all of the children on Christmas Eve in two and a half hours, my elf has an itinerary to guide Santa's visit. We start on the surgery floor, come down to the Pediatric Intensive Care Unit (PICU) where there can be children and youth into their mid-teens, and then cross over into the Neonatal Intensive Care Unit (NICU) where we find the newborns and the "preemies."

The big clock in the hall said 9:15 p.m. as Santa looked down the long hall and saw the NICU sign. Gently he started to ring his bells and then he could hear laughter and feel the excitement building at the end of the hallway. At the entrance Santa stopped, peeked his head around the door and called, "Merry Christmas! Ho, Ho, Ho!"

We are greeted by smiles, but also the reality that some parents are sitting there holding some pretty small children and others are watching the staff attend to their child through the ports of an incubator where heat and humidity are strictly controlled. The monitor lights of electrodes connected to the little bodies are blinking and audible beeping measures the children's vitals.

Santa walks into the room and turns to his right. A mother and father hold a little boy with beautiful, big blue eyes and a peaked cap. "Hi, Santa. This is Charlie."

This is Charlie's first Christmas story, told by his mother:

As new parents you get excited for everything. Your first ultrasound, first tiny baby clothes, first time seeing your child, every first milestone, and, of course, first holidays. Charlie was born on November 18, 2015, at 9:22 a.m. by emergency C-section at thirty-four weeks. He was lying on his umbilical cord, his heart rate kept dropping and after fifteen hours of flipping from side to side in the case room, our baby boy was coming, and quickly!

Delivery went smoothly, but we weren't finished with complications yet. As we were already aware, Charlie was born with gastroschisis; an abdominal wall defect that put his insides on the outside. Although we already knew of his condition we had no idea of how terrified we would be. Seeing him in his NICU bed for the first time was both the happiest and scariest moment of our lives. At only 4 lbs. 11 oz., Charlie was so tiny, so helpless and had such a long way to go. His surgery to insert his bowel took place on the morning of November 22nd and after waiting by the phone for four hours, we got the call that he was out and had pulled through perfectly. What a tough little guy Mommy and Daddy have! It was almost too hard to look at him directly after surgery and even in the week that followed. He had an oscillator machine in his mouth to help him breathe, IVs in his head, tubes coming out of both arms for fluids and a special port in his leg for bloodwork. The fluid he had retained after his procedure made our son barely recognizable.

As the weeks went on, Charlie made so much progress every day and it seemed like not much time at all until he was looking like himself again and one by one those tubes and IVs were coming out for good.

But we still had a lot of recovery to go. Because Charlie wasn't introduced to milk or feedings straight from birth, he had to be slowly fed through a small NG tube inserted in his nose, and, as we quickly learned, that can take a long time. However, Charlie loved his feedings, tolerated them incredibly well and even started a combination of tube and breastfeeding quite quickly. As his expected due date had been December 30th and he was doing so well, we tried not to get our hopes up but still had our fingers crossed that maybe, just maybe, he might come home a little early, December 24th, just in time for his first Christmas. Every day leading up to the holidays I asked if the nurses had any idea of when he might be discharged and every day after rounds we were told that he still needed a little more observation. As proud as we were that he was doing so well and had come so far, it was still disappointing to know that our baby wouldn't be home for his first Christmas.

On Christmas Eve, we finished our dinner with the family and got ready to head to the hospital. We had just picked up a tiny pair of reindeer sleepers and couldn't wait to put them on Charlie for his first Santa visit. All the while something still seemed so bittersweet and I couldn't help but think, this isn't how it's supposed to be. But I tried my best to put on a brave face. His daddy was a huge help with that, he's a lot stronger and more optimistic than I am!

As we got Charlie dressed in his pj's and little elf hat, I got more and more excited. I knew that Santa would be here soon and I couldn't wait for Charlie to see him.

Although he wouldn't even remember, he wouldn't have to miss out on anything. I never wanted him to miss out on anything. We were just tucking him in, warm and cozy, when we heard Santa's bells. You could feel the energy in the room and the whole mood lifted with the sound of the jingling and the 'Ho, Ho, Ho!' Every parent and nurse poked their head out the door to see where Santa was and we couldn't wait to catch a glimpse of him. And then there Santa was, making his way to Charlie's bedside as his first stop in the room.

When he picked him up and we saw that our baby was absolutely enthralled by Santa, everything else went away. There were no more beeping machines in the background, no more hospital pages, no more buzzing overhead lights. Just our son and Santa; like any other baby on Christmas Eve; like any other family. Santa rocked and cuddled Charlie, told him stories and talked to us, too, and our baby was in love. He adored Santa, and looked up at him with huge eyes while playing with his beard. Then, just as I thought it was time to take him back and go back to reality, I saw Santa give his helper a nod and she nodded back. We had no idea what was about to happen. We couldn't expect anything else as the whole experience had already done so much for us. Then Santa reached into his bag and unfastened the straps of a white fuzzy bear with a scarf reading 'Santa's Bear 2015.' At first, I didn't understand. I thought that he was letting Charlie play with this beautiful teddy for a little while, but then Santa and his helper told us the story of the special bears and how very special children are selected to receive them. Our Charlie was to be the luckiest of all the children there that night and the only one who was chosen to be Santa's elf and take his bear home forever.

Something came over me at that moment: a feeling that, even now, I still can't put into words. All I could do was cry. Every wish I had for our son's first Christmas came true that night, in that moment. He wasn't left out, he got a Christmas, and even more; someone else, complete strangers, saw something different in him, something extra special and they saw just how special he is.

Since that moment, we've made a promise that every year we're going to pass on something. Whether that is clothes, toys or spending time helping others. I don't know yet. But I do know that if Santa and his helper hadn't taken their time on Christmas Eve to make ours unforgettable, then nothing about our night would've been the same.

Love and generosity like that needs to be spread and always paid forward. Santa's visit showed us that there is still good in the world; that magic does exist, and from that night on we will always, always believe in Santa Claus.

Charlie came home to stay on January 5th and is a happy, healthy, sometimes handful of a baby boy. We cannot wait for next Christmas when we can show him his Santa photos, start telling him his story and let him know that not only is he special, he's an honorary elf!
Danielle

"The Teddy Bears' Picnic"

*If you go down in the woods today
you're sure of a big surprise
If you go down in the woods today you'd better go in disguise
For every bear that ever there was will gather there for certain
Because today's the day the Teddy Bears have their picnic
Every Teddy Bear who's been good is sure of a treat today
There's lots of marvelous things to eat
and wonderful games to play
Beneath the trees where nobody sees they'll hide
and seek as long as they please
That's the way the Teddy Bears have their picnic*

*Picnic time for Teddy Bears
The little Teddy Bears are having a lovely time today
Watch them, catch them unawares
and see them picnic on their holiday
See them gaily gad about
They love to play and shout
They never have any cares
At six o'clock their Mummies and Daddies will
take them home to bed
'Cause they're tired little Teddy Bears*

*If you go down in the woods today you better not go alone
It's lovely down in the woods today but safer to stay at home
For every bear that ever there was will gather there for certain
Because today's the day the Teddy Bears have their picnic.*

[1] "The Teddy Bears' Picnic"

Words and Music by John Bratton and Jimmy Kennedy

(c) 1947 (Renewed) WB MUSIC CORP. and EMI MUSIC PUBLISHING LTD.

This arrangement (c) 2016 WB MUSIC CORP. and EMI MUSIC PUBLISHING LTD.

All Rights Reserved Used by Permission

Reprinted by Permission of Hal Leonard Corporation

CONCLUSION

JOURNEY'S END

Thank you for joining Santa and St. Nicholas on their Christmas journey. While each story may have concluded with a teddy bear, it is my hope that you are thinking of the families in the stories that you have met along the way. Most of those who you met with Santa in the children's hospital on Christmas Eve did not expect to be there and their plans were turned upside down.

While you joined Santa and gave away teddy bears, you know now at the end of the journey, that we gave more than teddies. We gave courage, love and hope.

You have also met families who are looking to be part of the Canadian family, of your family and my family. Perhaps this journey will help us all widen our understanding of family.

Santa asked you to come with him through some uncomfortable doors and we shared those journeys as well. They are difficult visits but I find them much easier knowing that a very real Bishop of Myra, St. Nicholas has walked the path before us many years ago and is with me today as Santa makes his visits. Talk to your children about St. Nicholas.

Enjoy your family celebrations. I sincerely hope that you are reading this at a peaceful time, in a quiet place with cup of tea or a glass of wine.

Be grateful. And I ask you to consider one simple activity: please invite a child and host a teddy bears' picnic. We all have a bear somewhere and the child will never forget your kindness.

Bruce Templeton, 2016

Acknowledgements

This book is a memoir, and by simple definition contains the experience of the author. The stories are real and I should first acknowledge the families of the children and the organizations who allow Santa to be part of their lives.

My association with Santa goes back more than half of my life. I acknowledge my wife Paula who is with me through it all: in the helicopters, walking the parade routes and cobbling a tattered Santa together when he falls apart. Our doctor daughter Christina has been with me for many years on Christmas Eve in the hospital and she quietly gives me the confidence to deal with the challenges.

My editor for this book was Joan Sullivan, a well-known author and editor in her own right. The team at Creative Book Publishing is wonderful to work with, and what you hold in your hand is the result of the collaboration of some very talented people.

I would like to thank all of you, my readers.

Here are some of the people whose input has influenced this book: Pam Dooley, Alan Doyle, Donna Francis, Rick Hillier, Colleen Kennedy, Heather Martin, Joann Skinner, Susan McLeod, Darlene Didham, Leslie Goodyear, Danielle Pearce, Alice Power, Cindy Murphy, Suzanne Rendell, Joanne Snook-Hann, Todd Manning, Krista Spearns, Joan Sullivan, Janice Evans, Marian Templeton, Heather Walters, John Salmon, Philip Wenz, Kim Mallard, Jackie Caines, Chris Abbo Abbott, Trevor Murphy, Major John Goulding, Alisa Humber-Cutler, Mabs Leaman, Brenda Sheppard, Meighan Saunders, Debbie Clarke, Brad Michaels, Kerry Martin, Brian Bradley, Ann McCann, April Kenny, Fay Dawe Parsons, Bernadette Gentry, Gaylynne Lambert,

Scott Cluney, Christine Morgan, Ron Whiffen, Richard Rogers, Gerry Rogers, Jim McGrath, Denise Butler, Sister Diane Smyth, Tim Turner, Jerry Renda, Terry Reardon and Margaret Butt.